Choice Readings International Edition

Choice Readings

International Edition   Book 1

Mark A. Clarke
University of Colorado at Denver

Barbara K. Dobson
University of Michigan

Sandra Silberstein
University of Washington

Ann Arbor
THE UNIVERSITY OF MICHIGAN PRESS

Acknowledgments

The three of us began working together in the fall of 1973. As we near the millennium, we find we are still on speaking terms with each other, still listing our names alphabetically, and increasingly aware that the debt we owe colleagues, friends, family, and students has kept pace with inflation. We cannot possibly hope to repay all the people who have contributed to this work over the past four years, but civility demands that we acknowledge their efforts on our behalf. We want to thank the following individuals for continuing friendship, interest, critiques, and time.

We have benefited greatly from the classroom testing and detailed critiques provided by our colleagues: Hisako Kikuchi Travis, Seattle; Barbara Bell, Cindy Chang, Diane Clark, Ruth Jones, Barbara Lewis, Peter Messinger, Kimberly Newcomer, Jill Straight, and Tim Teigen at the University of Washington ESL Center, Seattle; Cynthia Nelson at Macquarie University, Sydney; Susan Borst and Janice Oldroyd at Spring International Language Center, Denver. Judy Bender, University of Colorado at Denver, tracked down potential readings. Special thanks to Sharon Tsutsui at the University of Washington for helping with this effort from the outset.

The UMP staff continues to exemplify professionalism, expertise, and goodwill. Thank you to Assistant Director Mary Erwin who calmly revises deadlines as fast as we miss them; to Managing Editor Christina L. Milton, whose editorial suggestions often verge on coauthorship; to Director Colin Day, whose leadership provides a healthy environment for creativity; to Pam Friedman, whose sleuthing and perseverance yielded many a missing citation.

And, of course, very sincere thanks and belated apologies to spouses and children, who undoubtedly wondered if we would ever get off the phone.

Ann Arbor, Denver, Seattle, January 1996

For this international edition, our debts to family, colleagues, and the University of Michigan Press continue unabated. To the list above, we add our thanks to the UMP's Kelly Sippell for conceiving of the project and ushering it through the production phases and Elizabeth Suhay for editorial assistance. Grateful acknowledgment also goes to the University of Washington's Cindy Chang for saving us from repeating our mistakes. As always, our families earn our deepest gratitude.

Ann Arbor, Denver, Seattle, December 1998

Grateful acknowledgment is made to the following for permission to reprint previously published material.

Allyn & Bacon for material from *The Macmillan Guide to Writing Research Papers* by William Coyle. © 1990 by the Macmillan College Publishing Company, Inc. Reprinted with the permission of Allyn & Bacon.

Associated Press for "Bugs Make Skin Crawl in Midwest," in *Denver Post,* May 30, 1990; "Graduation Speech Protested," in *Denver Post,* June 5, 1990; "High School Honors Not Always Key to Life Success," in *Denver Post,* June 19, 1991; and "Farmer Calls Hole His Home," in the *Seattle Times/Seattle Post-Intelligencer,* Sunday March 7, 1993. Reprinted with permission.

Bellevue Community College, Tuition Chart, Fall-Winter-Spring, 1994–95. Reprinted with permission.

Boston Globe for "Basic Science, Technology Leave Americans in Dark" by Richard Saltus, in *Boston Globe,* February 26, 1989. Reprinted with permission.

Diane J. Cole for "Stop Procrastinating," by Diane Cole, in *Working Mother,* December 1990. Reprinted with permission of author.

Cosmopolitan for "Japanese Marriage" by Judy Markey, in *Cosmopolitan,* August 1984. Reprinted with permission.

Denver Post for "Where to Go, What to Do," weekend section in *Denver Post,* May 17, 1991. © 1991 the *Denver Post.* Reprinted with permission.

Joseph Di Bona for "Brides and Grooms Wanted: Looking for a Wife in India—Not for the Faint of Heart," by Joseph Di Bona, in *Christian Science Monitor,* July 19, 1981. Reprinted with permission of the author.

Forth Worth Star-Telegram for "Lies Are So Commonplace, They Almost Seem Like the Truth," by Terry Lee (Goodrich) Jones, in *Seattle-Post Intelligencer,* October 29, 1990. Reprint courtesy of the *Fort Worth Star-Telegram.*

Grolier Publishing for "The Boy Who Cried Wolf," "Much Wants More," "The North Wind and the Sun," "Look Before You Leap," and "The Dove and the Ant" in *Tales from Aesop,* written and illustrated by Harold Jones. © 1981 Julia MacRae Books, a division of Franklin Watts. Reprinted with permission.

Henry Holt and Company, Inc., and the Estate of Robert Frost for "The Road Not Taken," by Robert Frost, from *The Poetry of Robert Frost,* edited by Edward Connery Lathem, © 1944 by Robert Frost. Copyright 1916, © 1969 by Henry Holt & Company. Jonathan Cape, publisher. Reprinted with permission.

Houghton Mifflin Co. and Frances Goldin Literary Agent, NYC for excerpts from *Families.* Copyright © 1990 Aylette Jenness. Reprinted by permission of Houghton Mifflin Company and Frances Goldin Literary Agent. All rights reserved. And for material from *Technical Writing,* by Frances B. Emerson. © 1987 by Houghton Mifflin Company. Reprinted with permission.

King Features Syndicate for six "Sally Forth" cartoons by Greg Howard. © 1990. Reprinted with special permission of King Features Syndicate.

Ann Landers and Creators Syndicate for "Adamant Smoker Says Stop Nagging," in *Denver Post,* June 18, 1990. © 1990. Permission granted by Ann Landers/Creators Syndicate.

Little, Brown and Company for excerpts from *The Rescuers* by Margery Sharp. Copyright © 1959 by Margery Sharp (Text); Copyright © renewed 1987 by author. By permission of Little, Brown and Company.

Macmillan USA for entries "compound" and "uniform." Reprinted with permission of Macmillan USA, a Simon & Schuster Macmillan Company, from *Webster's New World Dictionary,* Second College Edition. Copyright © 1980, 1979, 1978, 1976, 1974, 1972, 1970 by Simon & Schuster, Inc.

Pat Materka for "Think Positive!" by Pat Materka, in *Michigan Alumnus,* March/April 1992, and "After All, Tomorrow Is Another Day," by Pat Materka, in *Michigan Alumnus,* May/June 1990. Reprinted with permission.

McIntosh and Otis, Inc., for "The Case of the Buried Treasure," "The Case of the Dentist's Patient," "The Case of the Bogus Robbery," "The Case of the Blackmailer," "The Case of the Big Deal," "The Case of the Telltale Clock," "The Case of the Suicide Room," "The Case of the Locked Room," "The Case of the Murdered Wife," and "The Case of Willie the Wisp." © 1967 by Donald Sobol. Adapted from a story by Donald J. Sobol, from the book *Two-Minute Mysteries* published by Scholastic Book Services. Reprinted by permission of McIntosh and Otis, Inc.

Patrick Murphy for material from "The Adventures of Robin Hood" by Patrick Murphy, in *Ann Arbor Observer,* July 1991. Reprinted with permission.

Newsweek, Inc., for "The New Mating Games," by Barbara Kantrowitz, from *Newsweek,* June 2, 1986. © 1986, Newsweek, Inc. All rights reserved. Reprinted by permission.

Oxford University Press for entries "figure," "good," and "work" from *Oxford American Dictionary* by Carruth & Ehrlich Books, Inc. Copyright © 1980 by Oxford University Press, Inc. Used by permission of Oxford University Press, Inc.

Parents for "What's the Attraction?" by Ingrid Groller, in *Parents,* February 1990. Copyright © 1990 Gruner + Jahr USA Publishing. Reprinted from *Parents* magazine by permission.

Penguin Books USA, Inc. for excerpts from "A Laden Ass and a Horse" and "The Hare and the Tortoise," in *Aesop's Fables* by Heidi Holder, illustrator. © 1981 by Heidi Holder, illustrations. Used by permission of Viking Penguin, a division of Penguin Putnam Inc.

Penton Publishing, Inc., for "Procrastination" by James Braham, in *IndustryWeek* March 3, 1986. Reprinted with permission from *IndustryWeek,* March 3, 1986. Copyright, Penton Publishing, Inc., Cleveland, Ohio.

Random House for "How Nice to Have a Man Around the House—If He Shares the Chores" from *Inside America* by Louis Harris. Copyright © 1987 by Louis Harris. Reprinted by permission of Vintage Books, a Division of Random House, Inc. And for entries from *The Random House Webster's Unabridged Dictionary, Second Edition* by Random House, Inc. Copyright © 1997, 1996, 1993, 1987, 1983 by Random House, Inc. Reprinted by permission of Random House, Inc.

Research News for material from "Anxiety and Smoking," *Research News,* Sept.-Oct. 1990. © 1990 the University of Michigan. Reprinted with permission.

Science Service for "The Fall of the Forest" by Richard Monastersky, *Science News* July 21, 1990. Reprinted with permission from *Science News,* the weekly newsmagazine of science, copyright 1990, by Science Service.

Seattle Times for "The New Order," edited by John Gomes and Roger Ainsley, in *Seattle Times,* January 5, 1992. Reprinted with permission.

Silver Burdett Ginn for material from *A World View* by Clyde P. Patton, Arlene C. Rengert, Robert N. Saveland, Kenneth S. Cooper, and Patricia T. Caro. © 1988 by Silver Burdett Ginn, Simon & Schuster Education Group. Used by permission.

Alvin and Virginia Silverstein for excerpts from *Sleep and Dreams,* by Alvin and Virginia B. Silverstein. © 1974 by Alvin and Virginia B. Silverstein. Reprinted with permission.

Simon and Schuster for excerpts from "The Four Oxen and the Lion," "The Milkmaid and Her Pail," and "Belling the Cat." Reprinted with the permission of Simon & Schuster Books for Young Readers, an imprint of Simon & Schuster Children's Publishing Division from *The Fables of Aesop, Told Anew and Their History Traced* by Joseph Jacobs. © 1964 Macmillan Publishing Company.

Society for the Advancement of Education for "The 'New Father': No Real Role Reversal," *USA Today,* July 1989, and "Dumping Health Risks on Developing Nations," *USA Today*

(Special Newsletter Edition), April 1993. Reprinted with permission.

Sussex Publishers, Inc. for material from "The Eye of the Beholder," adaptation by Thomas F. Cash and Louis H. Janda, in *Psychology Today,* December 1984. Reprinted with permission from *Psychology Today Magazine,* Copyright © 1984 (Sussex Publishers, Inc.).

Time Life Syndication for "The World's Next Trouble Spots," *Time,* June 1, 1992. © 1992 Time Inc. Reprinted by permission.

TWA for the maps "TWA-Atlanta International Airport, Atlanta" and "TWA-JFK International Airport, New York." *TWA Ambassador,* April, 1994. Reprinted with permission.

United Press International for "Marriage Taking a Back Seat," in *Seattle Post-Intelligencer,* July 12, 1990. © 1990 United Press International. Reprinted with permission.

Universal Press Syndicate for the cartoon "Duffy" by Bruce Hammond. © Universal Press Syndicate. Reprinted with permission. All rights reserved.

University of British Columbia Public Affairs Office for campus map and accompanying text, "The University of Columbia: You'll Go Home a Different Person." Reprinted with the permission of the Public Affairs Office, University of British Columbia.

University of Michigan English Language Institute for questions adapted from the "Examination for the Certificate in English, 1994," by the English Language Institute, University of Michigan. Reprinted with permission.

USA Today for "Language Mirrors Immigration, Provides Key to Nation's Past, Present" and "Census: Languages Not Foreign at Home" by Margaret L. Usdansky, in *USA Today,* April 28, 1993. Copyright 1993, *USA Today.* Reprinted with permission.

Wadsworth Publishing Company for material from *The Research Paper: Process, Form, and Content, 6th ed.,* by Audrey J. Roth. © 1989 Wadsworth Publishing Company. Reprinted with permission.

Washtenaw Community College Admissions Office for Application for Admission. Reprinted with permission.

William Morrow & Company, Inc., for material from "A Real Soap Opera: Making Water Wetter" and "Tornado in the Drain" from *Rainbows, Curve Balls, and Other Wonders of the Natural World Explained,* by Ira Flatow. Copyright © 1988 by Ira Flatow. Reprinted by permission of William Morrow & Company Inc. And for material from *World of the Brain,* by Alvin and Virginia B. Silverstein. © 1986 by Alvin and Virginia B. Silverstein. Reprinted by permission of Morrow Junior Books, a division of William Morrow and Company, Inc.

World Future Society for "Aromacology: The Psychic Effects of Fragrances," *Futurist,* Sept.-Oct. 1990, "World Population Continues to Rise," by Nafis Sadik, *Futurist,* Sept.-Oct. 1990, "Levitating Trains: Hope for Gridlocked Transportation" by Richard Uher, *Futurist,* Mar.-Apr. 1991. Reproduced with permission from the *Futurist,* published by World Future Society, 7910 Woodmont Avenue, Suite 450, Bethesda, Maryland 20814.

Z Magazine for Cartoon by Kirk, July/August 1994.

Every effort has been made to trace the ownership of all copyrighted material in this book and to obtain permission for its use.

Contents

Contents / x

To Students: Read This First

Choice Readings is an intermediate-level reading textbook for students of English as a second or foreign language. The authors believe that reading is an active, problem-solving process. Effective readers must use a number of skills. To decide how to solve reading problems, readers must decide which skills or strategies to use.

Here is an example of active problem solving. Below are several sentences using the word *choice*. Next to them, is a list of dictionary definitions for *choice*. Take a few minutes to match the sentences with the correct definition.

__ 1. The authors of *Choice Readings* believe that reading is an active, problem-solving process.

    a. *adj.* of high quality, preferred

__ 2. In this textbook, you will have many *choices* in the types of reading you will do, the order in which you will read things, and the skills you will use to solve reading problems.

    b. *n.* the name of a wonderful ESL/ EFL textbook

__ 3. We have tried to choose the best reading passages we could find; we hope you enjoy these *choice* readings.

    c. *n.* options, decisions, selections

You probably did not have trouble finding the correct answers: 1-b, 2-c, 3-a. To do this task, you probably used several skills. You could use the context of each sentence and your knowledge of the world to get a general understanding of the word *choice*. The dictionary definitions gave you additional information.

Good readers decide why they are reading a particular selection before they read it, and they decide which strategies and skills they will use to reach their goals. They develop expectations about the kinds of information they will find, and they read to see if their expectations are correct. The exercises and readings in *Choice Readings* will help you become an independent, efficient reader.

When you look at the Contents page, you will notice that there are two kinds of units in *Choice Readings*. The odd-numbered units (1 and 3) contain skills exercises. These exercises give students focused practice in getting information from texts. The even-numbered units (2 and 4) give you the opportunity to interact with and form opinions about the ideas in longer texts.

Skills and strategies are introduced in early units and practiced throughout the book. The large number of exercises gives students repeated practice. Many teachers and students choose to move between skills and reading selection units; feel free to jump around in the book. You should not worry if you do not finish each exercise, if you do not understand everything in a reading selection, or if you have trouble answering a question. In fact, there may be more than one correct response to a question. The process of trying to answer a question is often as important as the answer itself. That process will help you improve your problem-solving skills and encourage you and your classmates to think about, talk about, and respond to our choice readings.

To the Teacher

It is impossible to outline one best way to use a textbook; there are as many ways to use *Choice Readings* as there are creative teachers. However, based on the experiences of teachers and students who have worked with *Choice Readings,* we provide the following suggestions to facilitate classroom use. First, we outline general guidelines for the teaching of reading; second, we provide hints for teaching specific exercises and readings in the book; and finally, we suggest a sample lesson plan.

General Guidelines

The ultimate goal of *Choice Readings* is to encourage independent readers who are able to determine their own goals for a reading task, then use the appropriate skills and strategies to reach those goals. For this reason, we believe the best learning environment is one in which all individuals—students and teachers—participate in the process of setting and achieving goals. A certain portion of class time is therefore profitably spent in discussing reading tasks before they are begun. If the topic is a new one for the students, teachers are encouraged to provide and/or help access background information for the students, adapting the activities under Before You Begin to specific teaching contexts. When confronted with a specific passage, students should become accustomed to the practice of skimming it quickly, taking note of titles and subheadings, pictures, graphs, etc., in an attempt to determine the most efficient approach to the task. In the process, they should develop expectations about the content of the passage and the amount of time and effort needed to accomplish their goals. In this type of setting, students are encouraged to offer their opinions and ask for advice, to teach each other and to learn from their errors.

Choice Readings was written to encourage maximum flexibility in classroom use. Because of the large variety of exercises and reading selections, the teacher can plan several tasks for each class and hold in reserve a number of appropriate exercises to use as the situation demands. In addition, the exercises have been developed to create variety in classroom dynamics. The teacher can encourage independence in students by providing opportunities for work in small groups or pairs, or by individuals. We recommend small-group work in which students self-correct homework assignments.

Exercises do not have to be done in the order in which they are presented. In fact, we suggest interspersing skills work with reading selections. One way to vary reading tasks is to plan lessons around pairs of units, alternating skills exercises with the reading selections. In the process, the teacher can show students how focused skills work transfers to the reading of longer passages. For example, Sentence Study exercises provide intensive practice in analyzing complex grammatical structures; this same skill should be used by students in working through reading selections. The teacher can pull problematic sentences from readings for intensive classroom analysis, thereby encouraging students to do the same on their own when difficult syntax impedes comprehension.

It is important to *teach, then test.* Tasks should be thoroughly introduced, modeled, and practiced before students are expected to perform on their own. Although we advocate rapid-paced, demanding class sessions, we believe it is extremely important to provide students with a thorough introduction to each new exercise. At least for the first example of each type of exercise, some oral work is necessary. The teacher can demonstrate the skill using the example item and work through the first few items with the class as a whole. Students can then work individually or in small groups.

Specific Suggestions

Choice Readings has been organized so that specific skills can be practiced before students need those skills for full reading selections. Although exercises and readings are generally graded according to difficulty, it is not necessary to use the material in the order in which it is presented. Teachers are encouraged:

a) to intersperse skills work with reading selections,

b) to skip exercises that are too easy or irrelevant to students' interests,

c) to do several exercises of a specific type at one time if students require intensive practice in that skill, and

d) to jump from unit to unit, selecting reading passages that satisfy students' interests and needs.

Skills Exercises

Nonprose Reading

Throughout *Choice Readings* students are presented with nonprose selections (such as maps) so that they can practice using their skills to read material that is not arranged in sentences and paragraphs. For students who expect to read only prose material, teachers can point out that nonprose reading provides more than an enjoyable change of pace. These exercises provide legitimate reading practice. The same problem-solving skills can be used for both prose and nonprose material. Just as one can skim a textbook for general ideas, it is possible to skim a graphic for the kind of information presented and for the main ideas. Students may feel that they can't skim or scan; working with nonprose items shows them that they can.

Nonprose exercises are good for breaking the ice with new students, for beginning or ending class sessions, for role playing, or for those Monday blues and Friday blahs. Because they are short, rapid-paced activities, they can be kept in reserve to provide variety, or to fill a time gap at the end of class.

Nonprose exercises present students with realistic language problems they might encounter in an English-speaking environment. The teacher can set up simulations to achieve a realistic atmosphere. The application exercise is intended to provide practice in filling out forms.

Word Study

Upon encountering an unfamiliar vocabulary item in a passage, there are several strategies readers can use to determine the message of the author. First, they can continue reading, realizing that often a single word will not prevent understanding of the general meaning of a selection. If further reading does not solve the problem, readers can use one or more of three basic skills to arrive at an understanding of the unfamiliar word. They can use context clues to see if surrounding words and grammatical structures provide information about the unknown word. They can use word analysis to see if understanding the parts of the word leads to an understanding of the word. Or, they can use a dictionary to find an appropriate definition. *Choice Readings* contains numerous exercises that provide practice in these three skills. These exercises can be profitably done in class either in rapid-paced group work or by alternating individual work with class discussion. Like nonprose work, Word Study exercises can be used to fill unexpected time gaps.

Guessing the meaning of an unfamiliar word from context clues involves using the following kinds of information:

a) knowledge of the topic about which you are reading,

b) knowledge of the meanings of the other words in the sentence (or paragraph) in which the word occurs,

c) knowledge of the grammatical structure of the sentence in which the word occurs, and
d) knowledge of discourse-level clues that can aid comprehension.

Context Clues exercises appear frequently throughout the book, both in skills units and with reading selections. Students should learn to be content with a general meaning of a word and to recognize situations in which it is not necessary to know a word's meaning. In skills units, these exercises should be done in class to ensure that students do not look for exact definitions in the dictionary. When Vocabulary from Context exercises appear with reading selections, they are intended as tools for learning new vocabulary items and often for introducing ideas to be encountered in the reading. In this case they can be done at home as well as in class.

Stems and Affixes exercises appear in both skills units and must be done in the order in which they are presented. The exercises are cumulative: each exercise makes use of word parts presented in previous units. All stems and affixes taught in *Choice Readings* are listed with their definitions in the Appendix. These exercises serve as an important foundation in vocabulary skills work for students whose native language does not contain a large number of words derived from Latin or Greek. Students should focus on improving their ability to analyze word parts as they work with the words presented in the exercises. During the introduction to each exercise, students should be encouraged to volunteer other examples of words containing the stems and affixes presented. Exercises 1 and 2 can be done as homework.

Sometimes the meaning of a single word is essential to an understanding of the total meaning of a selection. If context clues and word analysis do not provide enough information, it will be necessary to use a dictionary. We believe that intermediate students should use an English/English dictionary. The Word Study: Dictionary Use exercise in Unit 3 provides students with a review of the information available from dictionaries and practice in using a dictionary to obtain that information. Exercise 1 requires a substantial amount of class discussion to introduce information necessary for dictionary work.

Sentence Study

Sometimes comprehension of an entire passage requires the understanding of a single sentence. Sentence Study exercises give students practice in analyzing the structure of sentences to determine the relationships of ideas within a sentence. Students are presented with a complicated sentence followed by tasks that require them to analyze the sentence for its meaning. Often the student is required to use the available information to draw inferences about the author's message. Students should not be overly concerned about unfamiliar vocabulary in these exercises; the focus is on grammatical clues. Student errors often indicate structures that they have trouble reading, thus providing the teacher with a diagnostic tool for grammar instruction.

Paragraph Reading

These exercises give students practice in understanding how the arrangement of ideas affects the overall meaning of a passage. Some of the paragraph exercises are designed to provide practice in discovering the general message. Students are required to determine the main idea of a passage. Other paragraph exercises provide practice in careful, detailed reading. Students are required not only to determine the main idea of a passage but also to guess meanings of words from context, to understand specific details in the paragraph, and to draw conclusions based on their understanding of the passage.

If Main Idea paragraphs are read in class, they may be timed. If the exercises are done at home, students can be asked to come to class prepared to defend their answers in group discussion. One way to stimulate discussion is to ask students to identify incorrect responses as too broad, too narrow, or false.

The Restatement and Inference exercise is short enough to allow sentence-level analysis. This exercise provides intensive practice in syntax and vocabulary work as well as in drawing inferences.

Discourse Focus

Effective reading requires the ability to select skills and strategies appropriate to a specific reading task. The reading process involves using information from the full text and one's own knowledge in order to interpret a passage. Readers use this information to make predictions about what they will find in a text and to decide how they will read. Sometimes one needs to read quickly to obtain only a general idea of a text; at other times one reads carefully, drawing inferences about the intent of the author. An introduction to these approaches to reading is provided in Unit 1, and exercises throughout the book reinforce them.

Skimming is quick reading for the general idea(s) of a passage. This kind of rapid reading is appropriate when trying to decide if careful reading would be desirable or when there is not time to read something carefully.

Like skimming, *scanning* is also quick reading. However, in this case the search is more focused. To scan is to read quickly in order to locate specific information. When we read to find a particular date, name, or number, we are scanning. Skimming and scanning activities should be done quickly in order to demonstrate to students the utility of these approaches for some tasks.

Reading for thorough comprehension is careful reading in order to understand the total meaning of the passage. At this level of comprehension the reader has summarized the author's ideas but has not necessarily made a critical evaluation of those ideas.

Critical reading demands that readers make judgments about what they read. This kind of reading requires posing and answering questions such as *Does my own experience support that of the author? Do I share the author's point of view? Am I convinced by the author's arguments and evidence?*

Discourse Focus exercises provide opportunities for practice in all of these approaches to reading. The short mysteries can be valuable for group work since students can use specific elements of the text to defend their inferences. During group work, the diversity of student responses that emerges can reinforce the notion that there is not a single correct answer, that all predictions are, by definition, only working hypotheses to be constantly revised.

Reading Selections

Teachers have found it valuable to introduce readings in terms of ideas, vocabulary, and syntax before students are asked to work on their own. The section Before You Begin introduces the concepts and issues encountered in reading selections. After an introduction to the passage, several types of classroom dynamics have been successful with reading selections.

1. In class—the teacher reads the entire selection orally; or the teacher reads part, the students finish the selection individually; or the students read the selection individually (perhaps under time constraint).
2. In class and at home—part of the selection is read in class, followed by discussion; the students finish reading at home.
3. At home—students read the entire selection at home.
4. For additional suggestions using *Choice Readings* audiotapes, see the next page.

Comprehension questions are usually discussed in class with the class as a whole, in small groups, or in pairs. The paragraphs in the selections are numbered to facilitate discussion.

The teacher can pull out difficult vocabulary and/or sentences for intensive analysis and discussion *when they impede comprehension.*

Readings represent a variety of topics and styles. The exercises have been written to focus on the most obvious characteristics of each reading.

a) Well-organized readings with many facts and figures are appropriate for scanning and skimming. This type of reading can also be used in composition work as a model of organizational techniques.
b) If the reading is an editorial, essay, or other form of personal opinion, students should read critically to determine if they agree with the author. Students are encouraged to identify excerpts that reveal the author's bias or that can be used to challenge the validity of the author's argument.

c) Fiction and personal experience narratives lend themselves to an appreciation of language. Teachers often find it useful to read some of these aloud to heighten this appreciation.

d) Expository reading selections, such as popular science and social science articles, offer students the opportunity to focus on reading for thorough comprehension. Exercises that accompany these selections also encourage students to use their critical reading skills in evaluating and applying the detailed information presented in the texts.

Audiotapes

Cassette tapes are available for selected passages. These are indicated with a tape icon on the Contents pages and in the text at the heading for the passage. The tapes lend themselves to a variety of procedures. Students can listen on their own either at home or in a language laboratory, or recordings can become part of classroom activities. Teachers can play introductory paragraphs to help students enter a reading selection, or the entire passage may be played. Playing the tape through as students read a text for the first time can demonstrate the value of skimming. As a culminating activity, listening to the passage can allow students to appreciate the cadence of language they have studied.

Answer Key

Because the exercises in *Choice Readings* are designed to provide students with the opportunity to practice and improve their reading skills, the processes involved in arriving at an answer are often more important than the answer itself. It is expected that students will not use the Answer Key until they have completed the exercises and are prepared to defend their answers. If a student's answer does not agree with the Key, it is important for the student to return to the exercise to discover the source of the disagreement. In a classroom setting, students should view the Answer Key as a last resort to be used only when they cannot agree on an answer. The Answer Key also makes it possible for students engaged in independent study to use *Choice Readings.*

Sample Lesson Plan

The following lesson plan is meant only as an example of how goals might be translated into practice. We do not imply that a particular presentation is the only one possible for a given reading activity nor that the activities presented here are the only activities possible for achieving our goals. The lesson plan demonstrates how skills work can be interspersed with reading selections. Notice also that we have tried to achieve a classroom atmosphere that encourages individual initiative and group interaction. By integrating focused skill work with reading selections and by using activities that encourage students to debate answers and defend their opinions, we hope to create an energetic, text-based conversation.

The lessons described here would be appropriate for a class that had worked together for several weeks. This is important for three reasons. First, we hope that a nonthreatening atmosphere has been established in which people feel free to volunteer opinions and make guesses. Second, we assume that the students have come to recognize the importance of a problem-solving approach to reading and that they are working to improve skills and strategies using a variety of readings and exercises. We also assume that the class uses workshop formats and small-group activities for reading and writing instruction.

Although these lessons are planned for 50-minute, daily classes, slight modification would make them appropriate for a number of other situations. Approximate times for each activity are indicated. The exercises and readings are taken from Units 3 and 4.

Monday

Nonprose Reading: Campus Map (30 minutes)

a) The teacher asks how many students have used maps before and gets students to discuss the situations in which they use maps. They also discuss occasions on which they have used English language maps. Alternatives to maps are discussed. Maps represent just one way to find one's way around, and in many cultures, they would be used only as a last resort. The goal of this preliminary discussion is to pique students' interest and to help them consider alternatives to customary ways of getting places.

b) The teacher reads the directions aloud as students follow along. Everyone opens the foldout map at the back of the book. The teacher pauses, giving students a chance to focus on and examine the map. When they appear to be oriented, s/he directs their attention to the listing of places to go and things to do in Unit 3. S/he asks a few questions in an offhand manner to engage their interest: "Anything here that looks interesting to you?" "Does this look like an interesting place to go to school?" S/he does not actively seek answers to these questions but rather gives students time to explore.

c) S/he draws their attention to Part 1, reading the questions aloud and fielding answers in such a way that encourages students to participate. In general, this means that s/he remains somewhat noncommittal, saying such things as "Oh, do you think so?" and "Does everyone agree with that?" At times s/he will feign ignorance and ask students to convince her. When they get to question 4, s/he uses understanding acquired of individual students to engage them in banter about how they might spend their time if they were on the UBC campus for a few days.

d) S/he then quickly organizes them into groups of three and four, the membership of which s/he had determined before class. Students have ten minutes to work together to answer questions 5 to 12 in Part 2.

e) The teacher wanders around the room as the students work, talking with students, answering questions, encouraging an informal, information-seeking atmosphere in the classroom.

f) When most of the groups have finished, the teacher asks individuals to read items and give the answers their group came up with. They can confer with other members of their group as they give answers. The teacher routinely asks if the other groups agree with the answers. Discussion and differences of opinion are encouraged.

Reading Selection 1: Newspaper Article (20 minutes)

a) The teacher asks students to look at the newspaper page pictured there. S/he asks a few questions: "What is this story about?" "Who is Ernest Dittemore?" "What is he doing in the photo?" The teacher floats the questions and then steps back, allowing students time to muse and ponder.

b) S/he then gives them six minutes to do the Vocabulary from Context. The teacher gives the time limit to encourage students to work quickly, not because there is any inherent advantage in doing the exercise in a particular amount of time but because experience has shown that their work is more focused and effective when a small amount of pressure is applied. They are to write something in every blank. S/he encourages them to guess even if they have no idea about the meaning of the word; a wrong answer is better than no answer. The rule of thumb s/he follows is 30 seconds per item, but as s/he walks around the room, s/he notices how far they have gotten, and when most of the students have completed the items s/he calls, "Time!"

c) The teacher then gives them a few minutes to compare answers with a neighbor. They have done this many times in the past so they know that they are to justify their guesses with evidence from the surrounding text.

d) After most of the pairs of students have discussed the answers to the items, the teacher calls on students to read the sentences aloud and give their meanings for the italicized words. S/he encourages alternative guesses and helps the class work through the possibilities. S/he does not provide definitions; the goal of the activity is as much improvement of the students' guessing abilities as it is mastery of vocabulary.

e) They then turn back to the article. Because time is running out, the teacher decides to begin reading the story aloud while the students follow along in their books.

Homework: Time expires, and the teacher assigns the rest of the story to be read at home. S/he also asks them to do the Comprehension and Critical Reading exercises before they come to class and to read over the Discussion/Composition exercise.

Tuesday

Reading Selection 1: Newspaper Article (20 minutes)

a) As students begin to arrive, the teacher engages them in casual conversation about Ernest Dittemore and his unique living arrangements. S/he asks open-ended questions, encouraging students to speculate about Mr. Dittemore and his lifestyle.

b) When everyone has arrived, the teacher gives them time to compare homework answers with neighbors. S/he reminds them to use the text to support their answers. S/he wanders around the room observing and listening to the conversations.

c) After about five minutes, s/he calls the class to order and they work through the exercises. They follow a variety of formats for this sort of activity; in this case they proceed in fixed order around the room: A student reads the item and gives his/her answer. The teacher asks if everyone agrees, without indicating whether the answer is right or wrong. S/he encourages discussion and speculation. If everyone agrees, the next student takes a turn. Discussion of the Critical Reading exercise takes considerable time as students disagree about which adjectives accurately describe Mr. Dittemore. The teacher remains in the background as students talk, occasionally reminding them to use the text to support their answers.

Writer's Workshop: Supporting Your Opinion (20 minutes)

a) Because the discussion about Mr. Dittemore was so animated, the teacher decides to extend the time they spend on this. S/he asks students to select one of the statements from Discussion/Composition as a topic sentence for a paragraph. S/he then has them get into groups according to which statement they have selected and directs them to generate a paragraph supporting their point of view.

b) As students work, the teacher circulates and helps them with encouragement and tips. S/he reminds them of rules of thumb they have studied about paragraph development: making sure sentences relate to each other and to the topic sentence, distinguishing between fact and opinion, etc.

c) Time is running out. The teacher promises students time to finish the paragraphs tomorrow. S/he asks them to turn to the Stems and Affixes exercise.

Word Study: Stems and Affixes (10 minutes)

a) The teacher works through the chart of stems and affixes, definitions and examples, reading aloud, answering questions and eliciting additional examples from the students as s/he goes.

b) Students are given the remaining time to work on the exercises.

Homework: Stems and Affixes exercises 1 and 2.

Wednesday

Author's Chair: Ernest Dittemore Paragraphs (20 minutes)

a) As students enter the classroom, the teacher tells them to go straight to work on their paragraphs in their small groups.

b) As they refine the paragraphs, the teacher circulates, reminding them of the time.

c) When the groups have a respectable draft, s/he asks for a volunteer from each group to read their paragraph to the class. S/he asks the class to give the authors feedback on how effectively they have made their case, not whether they agree or disagree. S/he also comments on the paragraphs, calling attention to the occasional sentence that could be improved and commending them for points well made and vocabulary appropriately used.

Word Study: Stems and Affixes (15 minutes)

a) Students work in pairs and small groups to check answers to exercises 1 and 2. The teacher circulates to monitor conversations, check comprehension, moderate disagreements, etc.

b) The teacher asks if there are questions remaining about any of the items; a brief discussion of selected items follows.

Paragraph Reading: Restatement and Inference (15 minutes)

a) The teacher reads the directions and example for the Paragraph Reading exercise then gives students time to select their answers for the example paragraph.

b) The class compares their answers and the teacher leads the discussion as they compare their answers with the Explanation.

c) Students are given time to work on the paragraphs.

d) With five minutes left in the period, the teacher reconvenes the class. S/he asks for a volunteer to read the first paragraph and to give the answers s/he selected. Differences of opinion are moderated by the teacher; when students are not able to convince each other, the teacher asks one of the protagonists to check the key and explain the correct answer(s). (S/he uses the answer key sparingly and encourages students to exhaust their own strategies before they turn to it for confirmation of an answer. Students are to use the key for feedback on their efforts not to facilitate completing exercises.)

Homework: Finish the Paragraph Reading; come to class prepared to defend your answers.

Thursday

Paragraph Reading: Restatement and Inference (20 minutes)

a) As students enter, they are told to compare answers in pairs or small groups.

b) When all students are present, the teacher calls the class to order, and they check their answers to the paragraphs. Students volunteer for each item and follow a familiar routine: The student selected reads the paragraph aloud and identifies the answers s/he has selected. The teacher asks if everyone agrees. Discussion ensues as they work back and forth between the answers and the text. The teacher encourages students to explain their reasons for answers and to defend their choices by citing the text.

Reading Selection 2: Popular Social Science (30 minutes)

a) The teacher asks the class if they know what a lie is. S/he asks them if they ever lie. S/he smiles and nods as students exchange stories about friends who told outrageous lies and times when they "had to lie."

b) S/he then directs them to the Before You Begin questions under number 1 and gives them three minutes to answer them. As they finish, s/he asks students to compare answers with their neighbors. S/he interrupts the conversations to read number 2 aloud and instructs them to come to an agreement in their small groups about which items should be considered "little lies."

c) The students are caught up in the discussion, but the teacher calls them to order. S/he orchestrates the conversation but students do most of the talking. They read each item, declare it to be a "big" or "little" lie, and defend their answers. The teacher asks for comments, disagreements, or elaboration from the other groups. As the discussion gets livelier and livelier, s/he reminds them that a "lie" is a culturally loaded term and that different people will have different opinions about what constitutes a lie. S/he also reminds them that their task is to present their opinions as convincingly as possible.

d) With about ten minutes remaining in the class, s/he cuts off conversation, and asks them to turn to the Vocabulary from Context exercise 1. S/he reads the selection aloud while they follow in their books. Then s/he gives them a few minutes to jot definitions to the six words. When everyone has had a chance to guess the meaning of each word, s/he works with students to arrive at agreements on definitions.

Homework: Read "Lies Are So Commonplace, They Almost Seem Like the Truth"; complete Comprehension exercises 1, 2, and 3.

Friday

Reading Selection 2: Popular Social Science (30 minutes)

a) The teacher begins the lesson by reading the selection aloud or playing the tape as students follow along in their books.

b) S/he then asks them to turn to Vocabulary from Context exercise 2. S/he reads the paragraph in which the word is found, and students shout out the answer. Disagreements and confusions are handled as opportunities for conversation.

c) Next, s/he gives them a few minutes to look over the work they have done on the Comprehension exercises 1, 2, and 3. S/he then has them count off to form groups of four and five. They have ten minutes to compare answers to the questions and to arrive at a consensus on the answers. As they work s/he circulates. S/he reminds them that they need to defend their answers.

d) The teacher reconvenes the class, and they go through the answers one by one. As each item is answered s/he encourages conversation and disagreement.

Discourse Focus: Careful Reading/Drawing Inferences (20 minutes)

a) The teacher reads the directions aloud as students follow in their texts. S/he then reads Mystery 1 aloud and asks the question at the end. Students confer among themselves, and as a group the class arrives at the answer. The teacher facilitates the conversation and points out the additional clues at the end of the exercise.

b) S/he tells students they have ten minutes to read and answer as many mysteries as they are able.

c) Students spend the last ten minutes solving Mysteries 2 and 3.

Homework: None, if they have finished the mysteries; if not, do them at home. Have a nice weekend.

Several aspects of this lesson plan invite comment. You will have noticed a tendency toward informality and lightness in the way that the lessons are conducted. This reflects the temperament of the teacher and should not be construed as a necessary element of a successful reading lesson. We believe that each teacher has his or her own style, that techniques and activities must be selected and modified to accommodate that style, and that each class has its own personality.

The lesson plan represents an active, problem-solving approach to the teaching of ESOL reading that emphasizes communicative activities and results in the integrated use of reading, writing, speaking, and listening. Students are required to do more than merely read passages and answer questions. In most of the activities, we focus on "extending comprehension" through conversation and writing rather than merely "checking comprehension" through exercises. We work to create a classroom atmosphere that promotes risk taking in the use of language and in expressing one's own opinions.

The task at hand determines, to a large extent, what students do and how the teacher participates in class activities. We plan for many activities so that each day contains variety in terms of lesson content and classroom dynamics. In each lesson, the tempo and tasks change several times. In the course of a week, virtually all language and reading skills are practiced in a variety of contexts and with a variety of materials. This has important implications for the nature of the class and for the role of students, and teacher.

The classroom dynamics change to fit the task. Several of the lessons begin as class discussions in order to get students thinking about the content and to encourage them to develop reading strategies that are consistent with the material. This is the approach used with the campus map, for example. Small group work is used extensively because we believe that language is best learned in an interactive environment in which students are engaged in communicating with others. At times the teacher reads selections aloud as students follow along, while at other times s/he gives them time to read on their own.

Throughout the week, we have emphasized the importance of student initiative. Although the students work together a great deal, we want individual students to take responsibility for their learning and to develop their own inner criteria for the answers to questions and contributions to class discussion. Note, for example, the way that comprehension exercises are conducted. Students are asked to select the answers that reflect their understanding of the passages and to use text to defend their choices. In the Stems and Affixes exercise, the teacher introduces the exercise, but the students do the exercises and check their answers. In this way, the teacher emphasizes the importance of students' responsibility for, and control over, their work.

In this approach to teaching, the teacher's role varies according to the activity. During the Stems and Affixes exercise, the teacher functions as a facilitator, intervening only when necessary to keep the activity going, and as a teacher in clarifying linguistic points or giving examples. As the students work on their paragraphs about Ernest Dittemore, the teacher functions as facilitator, participant, and teacher. As facilitator, s/he organizes the writing workshop and author's chair, providing guidelines and orchestrating the conversations among students. As personal problems and solutions are discussed, s/he functions as a participant, exploring interesting issues with the students, expressing opinions just as the rest of the class does. And finally, as teacher, s/he helps with questions of grammar and punctuation and correspondence style.

Another important feature of the lesson plan is the opportunity provided to encourage students to exercise some choice in what they do and how they do it. As the teacher coaches them through vocabulary exercises and skimming and scanning work, comprehension discussions, and writing tasks, s/he constantly reminds students of a variety of ways that a task can be approached. Students come to establish expectations about texts and to select productive strategies to accomplish their goals. Just as the teacher provided a preview of reading selections and asked for student opinion on which to read first, s/he might introduce a text and ask the students how they plan to read it. A newspaper article will probably invite different reading strategies than a piece of children's literature.

Throughout the term, students are encouraged to shift gears, to vary their approaches to language tasks. As they become more proficient users of the language, they take more responsibility for what they read and write and for the opinions they express in conversations.

Discourse Focus

Reading for Different Goals

Good readers read differently depending on what they are reading and their purposes. There are four basic types of reading behaviors or skills: skimming, scanning, reading for thorough comprehension, and critical reading. Each is explained below, and exercises are provided to give you practice in each skill.

Skimming

Skimming is quick reading for general ideas. When you skim you move your eyes quickly to acquire a basic understanding of the text. You do not need to read everything, and you do not read carefully. You read, quickly, such things as the title and subtitles and topic sentences. You also look at pictures, charts, graphs, etc., for clues to what the text is about.

Use the page from the Friday edition of the *Denver Post* (p. 4) to answer the following questions. Move quickly from the questions to the page. Do not write out your answers completely; just make notes that will help you remember your answers. Your teacher may want to read the questions aloud as you skim to find the answers.

1. Why is this page called "Where to go? What to do?" _____

   How is the information organized? _____

   _____

2. What kind of information does it contain? _____

   _____

   Does anything here interest you? _____

   Are there other things that you might want to do on weekends that are not mentioned here? _____

   _____

3. Will this page contain information on renting an apartment? _____

4. Is there anything going on Sunday afternoon that you could do before going over to a friend's house for dinner?

_____

_____

Scanning

Scanning is also quick reading, but when you scan, you are looking for information about a question you want to answer. You are usually looking for a number or a word or the name of something. When you scan, you usually take the following steps.

1. Decide exactly what information you are looking for and what form it is likely to take. For example, if you want to know how much something costs, you would be looking for a number. If you want to know when something starts, you would be scanning for a date or a time. If you want to know who did something, you would be looking for a name.

2. Next, decide where you need to look to find the information. You would turn to the sports section of the newspaper to discover who won a baseball game, and you would scan the "C" section of the phone book for the phone number of Steven Cary.

3. Move your eyes quickly down the page until you find what you want. Read to get the information.

4. When you find what you need, you usually stop reading.

The following questions give you practice in scanning. Use the page from the *Denver Post* to answer the questions. Your teacher may want you to do this orally or by circling answers on the *Denver Post* page.

1. A friend is coming to town who likes jazz. Is there any jazz happening this weekend? Who? Where? When? How much does it cost?

_____

_____

2. You heard that there was going to be a car show in Denver this weekend. Is this true? _____

If so, when? _____ Where? _____

How much does it cost? _____

3. You like country music and notice that Merle Haggard will be performing. When will he perform?

_____ Where? _____ At what time? _____

How much will it cost? _____

Thorough Comprehension

When you read for thorough comprehension, you try to understand the total meaning of the reading. You want to know the details as well as the general meaning of the selection. When you have thoroughly comprehended a text you have done the following things.

1. You have understood the main ideas and the author's point of view.

2. You have understood the relationships of ideas in the text, including how they relate to the author's purpose.

3. You have noted that some ideas and points of view that were not mentioned were, however, implied by the author. This is called "drawing inferences."

4. You have understood most of the concepts in the passage as well as the vocabulary. This may require you to guess the meanings of unfamiliar words from context or to look up words in the dictionary.

The following questions give you practice in reading for thorough comprehension. Answer the questions according to your understanding of the page from the *Denver Post.* Your teacher may want you to work on these individually, in small groups, or in pairs. True/False items are indicated by a T / F before a statement. Some questions may have more than one correct answer. Others require an opinion. Choose the answer you like best; be prepared to defend your choices.

Look at the picture of the butterflies.

1. Where will "Ziegfeld: A Night at the Follies" be held? _____

2. T / F   "Ziegfeld" is a comedy performance without music.

3. T / F   "Ziegfeld" will be performed on three days.

4. T / F   You must pay $38 to see the show.

Critical Reading

When we read critically, we draw conclusions and make judgments about the reading. We ask questions such as, "What inferences can be drawn from this? Do I agree with the point of view?" We often do this when we read, but in some cases it is more important than others, as, for example, when authors give opinions about important issues or when you are trying to make a decision.

Use the page from the *Denver Post* to answer the following examples of critical reading questions. In later reading in this book, you will do other kinds of critical reading, making judgments about the written arguments. For the questions below, there is no single correct answer; readers' opinions will vary according to their experiences.

Where To Go, What To Do

FRIDAY

Clint Black

One of the hot new artists on the country music scene, **Clint Black**, will perform with one of country music's legends **Merle Haggard** and up-and-comer **Lorrie Morgan** at Red Rocks Amphitheatre. For ticket information, call TicketMaster at 290-8497.
Time: 7:30 p.m.
Tickets: $19.50

'Ziegfeld'

"**Ziegfeld: A Night at the Follies**" will be presented through Sunday at the Denver Auditorium Theatre. The comedy includes songs by Irving Berlin, Jerome Kern, Cole Porter and Harold Arlen. Call 893-4100 for tickets or for more information.
Time: 8 p.m. today and Saturday; 7 p.m. Sunday.
Tickets: $25-$38

Jazz clarinetist

Clarinetist Eddie Daniels will join the **Colorado Symphony Orchestra** for two concerts at Boettcher Concert Hall, 950 13th St. The program will include classical and jazz works under the direction of guest conductor Carl Topilow. For tickets or more information, call 595-4388.
Time: 8 tonight and Saturday.
Tickets: $8-$26

Sesame Street

Sesame Street Live presents "Silly Dancing" through Sunday at the Denver Coliseum. The show introduces the newest member to the Big Bird gang, Grundgetta, a match for Oscar the Grouch. Call TicketMaster at 290-8497 for ticket information.
Time: 10:30 a.m. and 7:30 tonight; 10:30 a.m., 2 and 5:30 p.m. Saturday; 1:30 and 5 p.m. Sunday.
Tickets: $9.50, $8.50, $1.50 discount for children 12 and under.

Bluegrass artists

Home on the Grange concert series presents top bluegrass artists including the **Bluegrass Patriots** and Pete and Joan Wernick performing at Grange Hall in Niwot. For more information, call 444-4537.
Time: 8:30 tonight and Saturday.
Tickets: $6

Stamp show

The **Rompex 1991 stamp show** will be held for three days at the Holiday Inn, I-70 and Chambers Road. Museum displays and exhibits from stamp collecting societies will be featured. For more information, call 755-3817.
Time: 9 a.m.-6 p.m. today and Saturday, 9 a.m.-4 p.m. Sunday.
Tickets: $1, children under 15 free.

'ZIEGFELD': A Night at the Follies will be presented through Sunday at the Denver Auditorium Theatre.

SATURDAY

Riff performance

Riff will perform with **LL Cool J** at Arnold Hall Theater at the U.S. Air Force Academy. Call 1-719-472-2472 for ticket information.
Time: 8 p.m.
Tickets: $18, $15, $10

Aybar concerts

Pianist **Francisco Aybar** will join the **Aurora Symphony** for two concerts at the Aurora Fox Arts Center, 9900 E. Colfax Ave. Aybar will perform Rachmaninoff's Piano Concerto No. 2. Call 361-2910.
Time: 8 p.m. Saturday, 2 p.m. Sunday.
Tickets: $6

Train rides

The **Georgetown Loop Historic Mining and Railroad Park** is open on weekends through May. Passengers may board in either Georgetown or Silver Plume. The train will run daily beginning Memorial Day and continuing through Labor Day. Call 670-1686.
Time: 9:20 a.m.-3:55 p.m.
Tickets: $5-$12.50

Pottery sale

Potters for Peace will hold its fourth annual benefit **pottery sale** at Clayton College, 3801 Martin Luther King Blvd. Works will be available from more than 300 potters. Proceeds will benefit potters in Nicaragua. Call 781-2035.
Time: 9 a.m.-6 p.m. Saturday and Sunday.
Tickets: Free admission.

Jazz concert

The **Ron Miles Trio Plus** will perform in the New Dance Theatre of Cleo Parker Robinson, 119 Park Ave. West. Featured performers include Andrew Cyrille on drums and Joseph Jarman on saxophone and flute. Call 758-6321.
Time: 8:30 p.m.
Tickets: $10, $8 students with ID

Model railroads

A **train show** will be held for two days in the Sheraton Hotel at the Denver Tech Center. Displays, running layouts and train sets for collectors, buyers and traders is offered. Call 696-1386.
Time: 10 a.m.-3 p.m. Saturday and Sunday.
Tickets: $5 per family, $4 per individual.

CARLA SCIAKY and Pete Sutherland will be in concert at Cameron Church at 8 p.m. Saturday.

Acoustic music

Swallow Hill Music Association will present an acoustic concert with **Carla Sciaky** and **Pete Sutherland** at Cameron Church, 1600 S. Pearl St. The concert will include works from Sciaky's latest album, "The Undertow." Call 777-1003.
Time: 8 p.m.
Tickets: $10, $8 Swallow Hill members.

Library party

A 25th anniversary celebration and groundbreaking party for the Arapahoe Library District's new main library will be held at the new site, South Holly Street and East Orchard Road. Free hot dogs, ice cream, cake and entertainment will be included. Call 798-2444.
Time: 11 a.m.-2 p.m.
Tickets: Free.

Breakfast jam

The fourth annual **Boulder breakfast jam** will be held at Boulder Reservoir. Performers include the Left Hand String Band, Mollie O'Brien and the Blue Tips, Big Head Todd and the Monsters and others. Call 449-6007.
Time: 8:30 a.m. to dusk.
Tickets: $15 in advance, $18 at the gate.

Battle of bands

The third annual **Battle at the Square band competition** will be held for two days at Heritage Square in Golden. Bands will compete at the levels of junior and senior high, college and semi-professional in several categories. Prizes will be awarded for best vocalist, drummer, keyboardist and guitarist. Call 674-3341, ext. 567.
Time: 10 a.m.-10 p.m. Saturday and Sunday.
Tickets: $5

Art auction

The third annual **Artists for Colorado Youth Art Auction** keyed to the theme "Passages: Art Today" will be at the Colorado History Museum, 1300 Broadway. A free preview reception will be available Friday. Call 832-9791.
Time: 4-8 p.m. preview Friday; 6-7:15 p.m. silent auction, 7:30-8:30 p.m. live auction Saturday.
Tickets: $25

Showhouse finale

This is the final weekend for the 16th annual **Junior Symphony Guild Showhouse** tours at 350 Humboldt St. The show features a classic Denver home with each room independently decorated by local interior designers. Call 722-4434.
When: 10 a.m.-3 p.m. Friday; 11 a.m.-4 p.m. Saturday and Sunday.
Tickets: $8

SUNDAY

Morning concert

The **Azusa Pacific University Choir and Orchestra** will perform at the Denver First Church of the Nazarene, 3800 E. Hampden Ave. The 150-member choir will perform a variety of classical and popular songs. A free Continental breakfast will be offered before the concert. Call 761-8370.
When: 8:45 a.m. breakfast, 9:45 a.m. concert.
Tickets: Free-will offering.

Help for kids

Colorado Kids Care and **Funplex** are teaming up to help homeless children by accepting donations of baby items including clothing, formula and diapers at Funplex, located at South Kipling Street and West Coal Mine Avenue in Littleton. Each person who brings a donation will receive a free activity pass to Funplex. For more information, call 934-0227.
Time: 11 a.m.-6 p.m.

Auto exhibit

The eighth annual **Concours d'Elegance auto exhibit** will be held in the north parking lot at University Hills Mall, 2700 S. Colorado Blvd. Rare Porsches, Maseratis, Jaguars and racing cars will be featured. All proceeds benefit Denver's United Cerebral Palsy Association. Call 355-7337 for more information.
Time: 9 a.m.-4 p.m.
Tickets: $5

Origami

The Boulder Public Library's Sunday Specials program is presenting an **origami workshop** in the Japanese Garden at the library, 1000 Canyon Blvd. Participants will learn to make birds, boats and other objects using the age-old Japanese paper folding techniques. Call 441-3100.
Time: 3 p.m.
Tickets: Free.

Honor Band

The **Colorado Honor Band** will perform a spring concert at Skyview High School, 9000 York St. in Thornton. Call 778-6693 for more information.
Time: 2:30 p.m.
Tickets: Free.

Weekend

Diane Carman
Entertainment Editor
Tom Walker
Assistant Entertainment Editor

Weekend is published every Friday. Send all correspondence to Weekend, The Denver Post, 1560 Broadway, Denver 80202. Phone 820-1452. Items for Calendar must be received at least 10 days prior to publication. Copyright 1991, The Denver Post Corp.

MERLE HAGGARD: Country music legend performs at Red Rocks tonight.

1. What types of activities and events appear to be important to people in Denver? _____

   _____

2. T / F   If you are interested in gardening, you won't want to miss the "bluegrass artists" Friday night in Niwot.

3. T / F   If you were interested in buying a used car, you should look at this page.

4. Read about the Sunday morning concert at the First Church of the Nazarene.

   a. What kind of music do you think they will be playing? _____

   b. T / F   The concert is free.

   c. T / F   This would be a good event to take a new friend to.

5. Note that on Sunday there will be an origami workshop in Boulder. Based on the description, what

   do you think origami is? _____

   What is a workshop? _____

6. Circle the items in the *Post* that you would be interested in doing or at least learning more about. With a classmate or two, discuss the items you have circled and decide on something you would like to do together.

Nonprose Reading

Airline Terminal Maps

Below are two maps from a Trans World Airlines (TWA) magazine. The maps are provided to passengers who are flying into the United States so that they will know how to get to the baggage claim area to pick up their suitcases, to another gate to catch another plane, and to the street to catch a taxi or bus.

Answer the following questions according to your understanding of the map. Your teacher may want you to work individually, in pairs, or in small groups. True/False items are indicated by a T / F before a statement. Some questions may have more than one correct answer. Others may require an opinion. Choose the answer you like best; be prepared to defend your choices.

Part 1: Getting Oriented

1. When you get off the airplane, what are some of the first things you need to do in the airport? Look at the maps. Do you find everything you would need, or is there missing information?

2. On the JFK map, find the rest rooms closest to terminal 4A, gate 32.

3. Circle the Immigration area for JFK and Atlanta.

4. Circle the baggage claim areas in both terminals.

Part 2: JFK International Airport, New York City, New York

Use the map of JFK (page 7) to answer questions 5 and 6. TWA uses terminals 4A and 4B at JFK International Airport. Most transatlantic flights arrive and depart from terminal 4A and most domestic (U.S.) flights operate from terminal 4B. The terminals are connected by an enclosed walkway and by a convenient shuttle bus operating between gates 21 and 17. The bus runs every ten minutes between the terminals between 3 P.M. and 8 P.M.

If you arrive at JFK on flight 841 from Rome, you might find yourself at terminal 4A, gate 30.

5. If you are flying to Denver, Colorado, from New York on TWA, which terminal will your flight probably leave from? _____ How do you get there? _____

6. Does the map tell you where to catch a taxi or bus to the city? _____ What can you do to get information about ground transportation? _____

From "TWA-Atlanta International Airport, Atlanta" and "TWA-JFK International Airport, New York," *TWA Ambassador*, April, 1994, 51–52.

Part 3: Atlanta International Airport, Atlanta, Georgia

Use the map of Atlanta International Airport (page 8) to answer questions 7 through 11.

TWA uses Concourse C, gates 15, 17, 18, and 20 at Atlanta International Airport. The concourse is connected to the airport terminal by a walkway, a moving sidewalk, and a train.

7. If you arrive at gate 17, and you leave in an hour from gate 20, how would *you* decide whether you have enough time to go into the terminal? _____

8. If the TWA representative at your gate cannot help you, where would you go to change your ticket?

   _____

9. T / F   The baggage claim area for TWA is located in the South Terminal.

10. T / F   If you want to get into downtown Atlanta, you must rent a car.

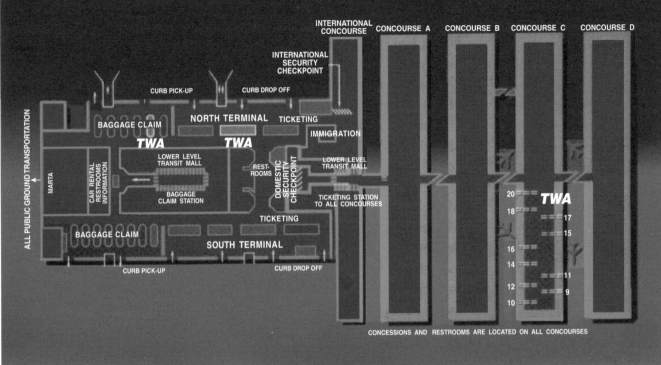

From "TWA-Atlanta International Airport, Atlanta" and "TWA-JFK International Airport, New York," *TWA Ambassador,* April, 1994, 51–52.

11. Which airport do you think is more convenient? Why? _____

_____

_____

Word Study

Context Clues

It is impossible to know the exact meaning of every word, but you can improve your ability to guess the general meanings of words from the words and sentences around the word. You have to use your understanding of English grammar and of the author's ideas and purpose. Here are some steps to follow in using context clues.

1. Use the meanings of other words in the sentence or paragraph and the meaning of the sentence as a whole to limit the possible meanings of the word.

2. Use grammar and punctuation clues to understand the relationships among the parts of the sentence.

3. Be happy with a general meaning of the word. The exact definition is not always necessary.

4. Teach yourself to keep reading even if you do not know the meaning of a word; it is not always necessary to know the meaning of all the words in a selection.

Example

Each of the sentences in this exercise contains a blank. You are to write a word in each blank using the context clues to guess the possible meanings of the missing word. You may not be able to think of a single word to put in the blank; in these cases, write a brief description or definition of the missing word. There is no single correct answer; the important thing is to improve your ability to guess.

---

1. Unlike his brothers, who are all very tall, Danny is quite _____.

2. George is a _____; he thinks only of money and will not spend a penny on anything if he can get it free.

3. The _____, like many other freshwater fish, is fun to catch and delicious to eat.

4. How could he be so stupid? He must have known that if he threw the ball against the window,

   it would _____.

5. I was tired and needed sleep, but the composition was due the next day, so I picked up a

   _____ and began to write.

6. Sandra is a loving mother; she _____ her daughter Maia.

7. Barbara rode her new _____ to work today. It is a bright red ten-speed, with hand brakes and rearview mirrors and a basket on the front for carrying things.

Explanation Check your guesses against the following words and explanations. Remember, there is no single correct answer for each item, just good guesses. In most cases, several words are provided, all of which fit the context. If you guessed one of these words or one similar in meaning, you have used the context clues correctly. If not, study the explanation to understand how to improve your guessing ability.

1. Unlike his brothers, who are all very tall, Danny is quite _____.

   short
   small
   squatty
   stubby

   Danny is the opposite of his brothers, and since his brothers are all tall, Danny must be short. The word *unlike* tells us about the relationship between Danny and his brothers.

2. George is a _____; he thinks only of money and will not spend a penny on anything if he can get it free.

   miser
   penny-pincher
   scrooge

   The semicolon (;) following the blank tells us that the two sentences are closely related. A miser is a person who does not spend money. *Penny-pincher* and *scrooge* are less common, but they mean the same thing.

3. The _____, like many other freshwater fish, is fun to catch and delicious to eat.

   cutthroat trout
   brown trout
   bass
   perch

   You probably did not write *cutthroat trout,* which is the word the author used. In this case, the comma (,) following the blank tells us that the word is defined or its meaning described in the words that follow, so we know that the missing word refers to a type of fish. Most native speakers would not know this word either. But since you know that the word is the name of a type of fish, you do not need to know anything else. This is an example of how context can teach you the meaning of an unfamiliar word.

4. How could he be so stupid? He must have known that if he threw the ball against the window, it would _____.

   break
   shatter

   You recognized the cause-and-effect relationship in this sentence. If you throw a ball against a window, it will likely break. This is an example of how the general meaning of a sentence defines the meaning of a word.

5. I was tired and needed sleep, but the composition was due the next day, so I picked up a _____ and began to write.

   pen
   pencil
   laptop computer

   The number of things that can be picked up in your hand and used to write with are few. You probably guessed pen or pencil immediately. Here, the relationship between the object and its purpose are so close that you have no difficulty guessing the meaning.

6. Sandra is a loving mother; she _____ her daughter Maia.

dotes on
(pours love on;
spends time with;
watches fondly)

Sandra is a loving mother. We all have an idea about how loving mothers treat their children, and this is the general meaning that we put in the blank. Punctuation helps us guess the meaning of the missing word. In this case, the semicolon (;) between the sentences tells us that the second sentence explains the first sentence in some way. *Dotes on* is not a common phrase, but when it is used it generally carries this specialized meaning. The phrases in parentheses may not fit in the sentence grammatically, but if you guessed the meaning of the missing word using these phrases, you know the meaning well enough to continue reading without going to a dictionary.

7. Barbara rode her new _____ to work today. It is a bright red ten-speed, with hand brakes and rear-view mirrors and a basket on the front for carrying things.

bicycle
bike

The description in the second sentence gives you all the information you need to fill the blank. This is an example of why you need to read beyond the word.

Exercise 1

In this exercise, do not *try to learn the meanings of the italicized words. Work to develop your ability to guess the meanings of the words using context clues. Read each sentence carefully, and write a definition, synonym, or description in the space provided. Do not leave any item without a guess. The only bad answer in this exercise is no answer.* Guess, guess, guess!

1. _____ We watched the cat come quietly across the field to where the bird *perched* on the wire. But just as it seemed that the cat would certainly catch him, he flew away.

2. _____ The Wilsons could not have children of their own, so they decided to *adopt* a baby.

3. _____ Elephants are in danger of disappearing completely. They are killed for their *tusks,* which people use to make jewelry.

4. _____ Goettleman was an angry old man, who could often be heard complaining and shouting and arguing about some part of modern life that he disagreed with. Just yesterday, for example, I heard him *railing* against women who work outside the home.

5. _____ The snake *slithered* through the grass.

6. _____   Ross is a very unpleasant person. The other day some of us were having a conversation in the hall when he came up and started arguing about politics and religion. As he became more and more excited, he pushed closer to me until I was backed up against the wall. Then he started *poking* me in the chest with his finger, as if he were punctuating a sentence on my shirt.

7. _____   My uncle is a *periodontist,* so when he comes to stay with us we have to be careful to brush our teeth after every meal. If we don't, he tells long stories about his patients, whose teeth have fallen out because they do not brush regularly.

8. _____   Just like his *taciturn* father, Jon rarely says anything at family gatherings.

9. _____   After not eating all day, Joyce was *ravenous.* She wanted to eat everything in sight.

10. _____   Eating a lot of rich food is unhealthy. The doctor told John he would have to *curb* his eating if he did not want to risk heart disease.

Word Study

Stems and Affixes

Using context clues is one way to discover the meaning of an unfamiliar word. Another way is word analysis. In word analysis, you look at the meanings of parts of a word. Many English words have been formed by combining parts of older English, Greek, and Latin words. If you know the meanings of some of these word parts, you can often guess the meaning of an unfamiliar English word, especially in context.

Think, for example, about the word *report*. *Report* is formed from *re*, which means *back*, and *port*, which means *carry*. *Scientist* comes from *sci*, which means *know* and *ist*, which means *one who*.

Port and *sci* are called stems. A stem is the basic part on which groups of related words are built. *Re* and *ist* are called affixes, that is, word parts that are attached to stems. Affixes like *re* that are attached to the beginnings of stems are called prefixes. Affixes attached to the ends of stems, like *ist,* are called suffixes. Generally, prefixes change the meaning of a word, and suffixes change its part of speech. Here are some more examples:

Stem	pay (verb)	honest (adjective)
Prefix	*re*pay (verb)	*dis*honest (adjective)
Suffix	*re*pay*ment* (noun)	*dis*honest*ly* (adverb)

Word analysis is not always enough to give you the exact definition of a word you find in a reading passage, but often, if you use context clues too, it will help you to understand the general meaning. It will let you continue reading without stopping to use a dictionary.

In this unit, you will work with a group of common prefixes. In later units, you will study stems, suffixes, and other prefixes.

Below is a chart showing some common prefixes that indicate *amount* or *number.* Next to each prefix is its meaning and words that include that prefix. Study the chart. Your teacher may ask you to give examples of other words you know that include these prefixes. Then, do the exercises that follow.

semi-	half	semicircle, semisweet
mono-	one	monarch, monopoly
uni-	one	unite, universe
bi-	two	bicycle, binary
tri-	three	triangle, triple
multi-	many, several	multiple, multiply
poly-	many, more than one	polytechnic, polynomial

Exercise 1

Use the chart to help you answer these questions. Your teacher may want you to do this exercise orally or in small groups.

1. A person who speaks only one language is monolingual.

   A person who speaks two languages is _____.

   A person who speaks three languages is _____.

2. Match each word with the picture it describes:

___ unicycle, ___ bicycle, ___ tricycle.

a.   b.   c.

3. a. When Leslie was 43, she had to get new eyeglasses so that she could see clearly both near and far. Her eye doctor told her she should buy bifocal glasses. What do bifocals look like? Draw a picture below.

   b. Some people even need to wear trifocals. What do trifocal glasses look like? Draw a picture below.

4. *Monogamy* means having only one marriage partner at a time. In the United States, monogamy is legal, but polygamy is against the law. What do you think *polygamy* means?

_____

5. *Car, man, book,* and *shop* are monosyllabic words because each has only one syllable. Circle all of the words in the following list that are polysyllabic.

| automobile | truck | computer | woman |
| television | sister | son | syllable |

6. Binoculars are an instrument used to see things far away. Which of these two pictures do you think shows a pair of binoculars?

a.   b.

7. Draw a picture of a triangle. Use word analysis to explain the meaning of triangle.

   _____

8. Which of these triangles do you think is an equilateral triangle? (Hint: *later* is a stem that means *side.*)

   a.   ◹   b.   △   c.   ◿

9. Some factory workers know how to use special, complicated machines. Others work on the simpler machines. Which kind of worker is called "skilled," and which kind of worker is called "semiskilled"?

   _____

   _____

10. In a hospital, rooms for only one patient are called private rooms. A room for many patients is called a ward. What are semiprivate rooms?

   _____

11. California is a multicultural state because of the large number of citizens from Latin America and Asia and other areas who live there. Describe what *multicultural* means.

   _____

12. The United States is a multiracial society. What does *multiracial* mean? _____

   _____

13. Twins are born about one time out of every 90 births, but triplets are much more unusual. What are triplets?

   _____

   _____

14. Many people, for example, police officers and soldiers, must wear uniforms when they are working.

   Use word analysis to explain the meaning of *uniform.* _____

   _____

15. Would you rather be a millionaire or a multimillionaire? Why? _____

_____

16. The United States was established in 1776. It celebrated its centennial in 1876. When did it

celebrate its bicentennial? _____

17. What would a multicolored shirt look like? Are you wearing one now? _____

_____

18. To keep her camera absolutely still, the photographer put her camera on a tripod. What is a tripod?

(Hint: *pod* is a stem meaning *foot*.) _____

_____

19. Which of these circles is bisected? (Hint: It is the picture that shows semicircles.)

a.　　　　　　　　　　b.　　　　　　　　　　c.

Exercise 2

Word analysis can help you to guess the meaning of unfamiliar words. Using context clues and what you know about prefixes, write a definition, synonym, or description of the italicized words.

1. _____ The magazine used to be published only once a year, but now it is printed *semiannually.*

2. _____ The new school has 20 classrooms, a library, an office area, and a large *multipurpose* room that can be used as a lunchroom, gymnasium, and theater.

3. _____ The English actor's *monocle* hung on a string around his neck. When he read, he held it to his eye.

4. _____ Bill hopes he will get the new job he applied for. The new salary would be *triple* the amount of money he makes now.

5. _____ Many people never expected to see the *unification* of West Germany and the German Democratic Republic.

6. _____ Al should not be in the choir; he sings in a *monotone.*

7. _____ This team will probably win the *semifinal* game, but I would be very surprised if the players are good enough to win the final, championship game tomorrow.

8. _____ According to the *bilateral* trade agreement, both countries will sell more of each other's products.

9. _____ The bank wanted to build a *multistory* building downtown, but the people of the small town did not want such a tall building on Main Street.

10. _____ In the *semidarkness* of the theater, I had a hard time finding my seat.

Sentence Study

Introduction

When you have difficulty understanding a passage, just reading further will often make the passage clearer. Sometimes, however, comprehension of an entire passage depends on your being able to understand a single sentence. Sentences that are very long, sentences that have more than one meaning, or sentences that contain difficult grammatical patterns often cause comprehension problems for readers. The Sentence Study exercise that follows as well as similar ones in later units helps you practice strategies for understanding difficult sentences.

    Although there is no easy formula for understanding complicated sentences, you should keep the following points in mind.

1. Try to determine what makes the sentence difficult.

   a. If the sentence contains a lot of difficult vocabulary, you may be able to understand it without knowing the meaning of every word. Try crossing out unfamiliar vocabulary:

   > It's a wonderful world that we live in—a world filled with rainbows and rockets, with ~~echoes and~~ electric ~~sparks,~~ with ~~atomic particles and~~ planets, with ~~invisible~~ forces ~~and vibrations~~ that affect us without our even knowing they exist.

   b. If the sentence is very long, try to break it up into smaller parts:

   > It's a wonderful world that we live in. The world is filled with rainbows and rockets. It is filled with echoes and electric sparks. It is filled with atomic particles and planets. It is filled with invisible forces and vibrations. These forces and vibrations affect us without our even knowing they exist.

   c. Also, if the sentence is very long, try to determine which parts of the sentence express specific details supporting the main idea. Often clauses that are set off by commas or dashes, or introduced by words like *which, who, that,* are used to introduce extra information or to provide supporting details. Try crossing out the supporting details in order to determine the main idea:

   > Our world—~~filled as it is with rainbows and rockets, with echoes and electric sparks, with atomic particles and planets, with invisible forces and vibrations that affect us without our even knowing they exist~~—is truly marvelous.

Be careful! A good reader reads quickly but accurately.

2. Learn to recognize important grammatical and punctuation clues that can change the meaning of a sentence.

   a. Look for single words and affixes that can change the entire meaning of a sentence:

   > Snowstorms are *not un*common.
   > The *average* daytime *high* temperature is *approximately* 56°.

b. Look for punctuation clues:

Jane writes ☺poetry☺ every morning.
Peter said, "Ron was elected president⑦"

Note that all of the italicized words or affixes and the circled punctuation above affect the meaning of the sentences; if any of these are left out, the meaning of the sentence changes.

c. Look for key words that tell you of relationships within a sentence:

The school has grown *from* a small building holding 200 students *to* a large institute that educates 4,000 students a year.

From . . . to indicates the beginning and end points of something (here, the growth of the school).

Many people feel that he is *not only* a wonderful researcher and writer *but also* a fine teacher.

Not only . . . but also indicates that both parts of the sentence are of equal importance.

In order to receive a grade in this course, you will need to finish each of the five assignments.

In order to is like *if;* it indicates that some event must occur before another event can take place.

He thought he would have to apologize to each of his brothers and sisters; *instead* they arrived at his house with presents.

Instead indicates that something unexpected happened.

As a result of all of the newspaper and television attention, the problem of the rain forest has become well known.

As a result of indicates a cause-and-effect relationship. The clause that follows *as a result of* is the cause of some event. The newspaper and television attention is the *cause;* the fact that the problem is now well known is the *effect.*

Because of these phenomena, which include rainbows and rockets, echoes and electric sparks, atomic particles and planets, and invisible forces and vibrations that affect us without our even knowing they exist, our world is a rich and wonderful place to explore.

Because of indicates a cause-and-effect relationship. The world is wonderful to explore as a result of these phenomena. The information between the word *which* and the final comma (,) refers to these phenomena.

Apart from the fact that he had traveled in that part of the world, there was no reason to think that he could speak the language.

In this sentence, *apart from* indicates that there is no other reason except that one. It means "except for."

Despite what many people believe, writing is more than a matter of putting one's ideas into words.

Despite indicates that the second part of the sentence will not agree with the first.

d. Look at the pronouns in the sentence. Pronouns are words (like *he, she, it, their, those*) that refer to some person, some thing, or some idea expressed elsewhere in the sentence. Try to determine exactly what person, what thing, or what idea each pronoun refers to.

Seventeen million people in the United States, more than half of all the people who speak a language other than English, speak Spanish. *That* is ten times as many as speak French.

Sentence Study

Comprehension

Read the following sentences carefully. The questions that follow are designed to test your comprehension of complex grammatical structures. Select the best answer.

Example

Cliff said he doesn't mind going to the grocery store if his roommate is too busy to go tonight.

We know that . . .

___ a. Cliff is too busy to go.

___ b. Cliff doesn't want to go.

___ c. Cliff's roommate is too busy to go.

___ d. Cliff may go to the store.

Explanation

___ a. According to the sentence, the person who might be too busy to go is Cliff's *roommate,* not Cliff.

___ b. The sentence says that Cliff "doesn't mind going," that he is willing to go. It does not say Cliff doesn't want to go to the store.

___ c. The sentence says "*if* his roommate is too busy." *If* indicates that the roommate may or may not be too busy. We don't know that he is too busy.

✓ d. The sentence says that Cliff is willing to go to the store if his roommate doesn't go, so we know that Cliff may go to the store.

---

1. and 2. Mrs. Dawson, who had just gone upstairs to change clothes, heard a sudden shout as she passed the old lady's door.
   Who shouted?
   ___ a. Mrs. Dawson
   ___ b. the old lady
   ___ c. We don't know.
   ___ d. Someone who had just gone upstairs.

Who was passing outside the door?
___ a. Mrs. Dawson
___ b. the old lady
___ c. someone who shouted
___ d. We don't know.

3. Albert was sitting next to Julia in the outer office when Alice returned after her meeting with Miss Cain.
Who had a meeting?
___ a. Albert and Julia
___ b. Julia and Miss Cain
___ c. Julia and Alice
___ d. Alice and Miss Cain

4. Joan, following the instructions of the new manager, took a calculator from the desk drawer and started to work out the new monthly rent figures for Mrs. Koester's and Mrs. Pye's rooms.
Who was doing the calculations?
___ a. Joan
___ b. the manager
___ c. Mrs. Koester
___ d. Mrs. Pye

5. If it wasn't bad enough that Kevin left the dinner early, I found out that he left with my coat instead of his.
What do we definitely know about Kevin?
___ a. He ate dinner early.
___ b. He should have left early.
___ c. It wasn't bad that he left.
___ d. He left his coat.

6. and 7. Other wildlife in which Charles was particularly interested and which he worked to save with the World Wildlife Fund were the Javan bison in Indonesia and the Tamaraw buffalo and the monkey-eating eagle (the largest eagle in the world), both of which are found in the Philippines.
Which animals are found in the Philippines?
___ a. the monkey-eating eagle and the world's largest eagle
___ b. the Tamaraw buffalo and the monkey-eating eagle
___ c. the Javan bison and the world's largest eagle
___ d. the Javan bison and the monkey-eating eagle

What did Charles do?
___ a. He worked to help animals.
___ b. He tried to save the World Wildlife Fund.
___ c. He discovered the largest eagle in the world.
___ d. He found Tamaraw buffalo in the Philippines.

8. If any final proof were needed of Joanna's remarkable abilities, it could be found in the way she performed on the difficult three-hour entrance examination.
   How did Joanna do on the examination?
   __ a. She did very well.
   __ b. She found the examination difficult.
   __ c. She could do all except the final proof.
   __ d. After three hours she hadn't finished.

9. Ms. Haar announced the winner of the contest once Mr. Wilson had arrived.
   What happened first?
   __ a. The winner was announced.
   __ b. Mr. Wilson arrived.
   __ c. Mr. Wilson won the contest.
   __ d. Ms. Haar won the contest.

10. Obviously, there was a tremendous amount of research that needed to be done, and that would require more money than was available by way of government funding.
    What was money needed for?
    __ a. to study government funding
    __ b. to get government funding
    __ c. to conduct research
    __ d. to repay the government

Paragraph Reading

Main Idea

In this exercise, you will practice finding the main idea of a paragraph. Being able to understand the main idea of a passage is a very useful reading skill to develop. It is a skill you can apply to any kind of reading. For example, when you read for enjoyment or for general information, it is probably not important to remember all the details of a passage. Instead, you want to quickly discover the general message—the main idea of the passage. For other kinds of reading, such as reading textbooks, you need both to determine the main ideas and to understand how they are developed.

The main idea of a passage is the thought that is in the passage from the beginning to the end. In a well-written paragraph, most of the sentences support, describe, or explain the main idea. It is sometimes stated in the first or last sentence of the paragraph. Sometimes the main idea must be inferred; it is not stated.

In order to determine the main idea of a piece of writing, you should ask yourself what idea is common to most of the text. What is the idea that connects the parts to the whole? What opinion do all the parts support? What idea do they all explain or describe?

Read the following paragraphs quickly to discover the main idea. Remember, don't worry about the details in the paragraphs. You only want to determine the general message. After you read each paragraph, circle the letter next to the sentence that best expresses the main idea.

Study the example paragraph carefully before you begin. When you have finished, your teacher may want you to work in small groups for discussion.

Example

To scan is to look for specific information quickly without reading word by word. You have to know what you're looking for before you begin. When you scan, look for key words, names, dates, or other specifics that mean you have found the information you are looking for. Don't stop to read everything on a page slowly and carefully. Instead, scan until you come to the information you need; then read carefully.

Which sentence best states the main idea of the paragraph?

___ a. Scanning is reading quickly to find specific information.

___ b. Before you read a passage, you should scan it.

___ c. It is not a good idea to read word by word.

___ d. Scanning is a useful reading skill.

Study the explanations following to understand how these sentences relate to the paragraph.

Example paragraph adapted from *The Research Paper: Process, Form, and Content,* by Audrey J. Roth, 6th ed. (Belmont, CA: Wadsworth, 1989), 112.

Explanation   ✓ a. This statement, a brief explanation of the process of scanning, is the main idea. All the other sentences in the paragraph give more details about the process of scanning—what it is and how to do it.

___ b. The paragraph does not say or imply that we should always scan a passage before reading it, so this statement is false. Therefore, it cannot be the main idea.

___ c. This statement is too narrow to be the main idea. It talks only about a part of the scanning process. It does not tell about the whole process of scanning that is described in the paragraph.

___ d. This statement is too general. Although it is true, the focus of the paragraph is more specific. The purpose of the paragraph is to describe the process of scanning.

Paragraph 1   A *process* is a natural series of actions and reactions that leads to specific results. All of us participate in a variety of processes every day. We digest our food, heal ourselves by making new skin cells, distribute resources through our bodies by breathing, and use our five senses. Natural processes go on all around us as well. Plants produce their own food through photosynthesis, storms build and move, volcanoes erupt, and fertilized eggs mature—the list seems endless.

Which sentence best states the main idea of the paragraph?

___ a. We all take part in many processes every day.

___ b. Natural processes that go on around us include photosynthesis.

___ c. A series of actions and reactions that leads to certain results is called a process.

___ d. Natural processes take place within our bodies.

Paragraph 1 from *Technical Writing,* by Frances B. Emerson (Boston: Houghton Mifflin, 1987), 170.

Paragraph 2   "How will it play in Peoria?" This question was asked in the United States in the 1920s when singers, dancers, and other entertainers performed in traveling musical shows. Performers thought that if the citizens of a typical U.S. town such as Peoria, Illinois, liked their show it would probably be popular across the country. If Peorians disliked it, the entertainers believed the show would fail. This "Peoria test" is still applied to the people of the state of Illinois. Illinoisans' likes and dislikes seem to mirror those of people across the land. Perhaps this is true because of Illinois' central location; it is a crossroads between east and west, north and south. Or perhaps it is because Illinoisans come from such different backgrounds and follow such a wide variety of lifestyles.

Which sentence best states the main idea of the paragraph?

___ a. Illinois is located in the central part of the United States.

___ b. Illinoisans come from different backgrounds.

___ c. The "Peoria test" is the name of a famous show.

___ d. Illinoisans' opinions seem to mirror the beliefs of people throughout the United States.

Paragraph 3   If you ask most people to explain why they like someone when they first meet, they'll tell you it's because of the person's personality, intelligence, or sense of humor. But they're probably wrong. The characteristic that most impresses people when meeting for the first time is physical appearance. Although it may seem unfair, attractive people are frequently preferred over less attractive ones.

Which sentence best states the main idea of the paragraph?

___ a. Judging people by their appearance is unfair.

___ b. Physical appearance is more important to what we think of others than we believe it is.

___ c. Personality, intelligence, and sense of humor are important in deciding whether you like someone or not.

___ d. Most people deceive themselves.

___ e. People should spend more time combing their hair.

Paragraph 2 from *America the Beautiful: Illinois,* by R. Conrad Stein (Chicago: Childrens Press, 1987), 7.
Paragraph 3 from "The Eye of the Beholder," by Thomas F. Cash and Louis H. Janda, *Psychology Today,* December 1984. Reprinted in *Our Times: Readings from Recent Periodicals,* by Robert Atwan (New York: St. Martin's, 1989).

Paragraph 4 All communication is a two-way process involving a speaker or writer and listeners or readers (the audience). In written communication, because the audience is not present, the audience is easy to ignore. However, the kind of audience you write for determines what you write and how you write. In describing the World Series baseball championship to a British reader, you would have to include definitions, explanations, and facts that a reader in the United States would not need. Similarly, if you write about cricket (a British sport) for an audience in the United States, you would need to include a lot of basic information. If you wrote about the international banking systems for bankers, your language and information would be more technical than in a paper written for readers who don't know much about the subject. A discussion of acid rain written for an audience of environmentalists would be quite different from one written for factory owners.

Which sentence best states the main idea of the paragraph?

___ a. Communication is a process that involves speakers and writers.

___ b. British readers would need special information to understand an article on the World Series.

___ c. Listeners and readers are called the audience.

___ d. It is important to consider your audience when you write.

Paragraph 5  Researchers at the University of Michigan are studying the effects of nicotine on the brain. Nicotine is the major drug in cigarettes. The scientists' long-term goal is to improve methods for helping people quit smoking. Recently they have found that cigarettes give several "benefits" to smokers that may help explain why quitting smoking is so hard. The nicotine in cigarettes seems to help smokers with problems of daily living. It helps them feel calm. Nicotine also causes short-term improvements in concentration, memory, alertness, and feelings of well-being.

Which sentence best states the main idea of the paragraph?

___ a. Researchers at the University of Michigan are studying how to help smokers stop smoking.

___ b. Nicotine improves concentration, memory, and alertness.

___ c. Some "benefits" of smoking may help explain why smokers have a hard time quitting.

___ d. Researchers at the University of Michigan have developed a new program to help people stop smoking.

Paragraph 4 from *The Macmillan Guide to Writing Research Papers,* by William Coyle (New York: Macmillan, 1990), 8.
Paragraph 5 adapted from "Anxiety and Smoking," *Research News,* September–October, 1990, 22.

Paragraph 6   The United States faces a transportation crisis. U.S. highways and airways are getting more and more crowded. In the next 20 years, the time that automobile drivers lose because of crowded highways is expected to increase from 3 billion to 12 billion hours a year. During the same time period, the number of airplane flights with delays of more than eight minutes is predicted to triple. For both highway and air travel, the estimated cost of delay to passengers will rise from $15 billion a year today to $61 billion 20 years from now.

Which sentence best states the main idea of the paragraph?

___ a. Airplanes will not be delayed as much as cars will be.

___ b. Transportation problems in the United States are increasing.

___ c. Twenty years from now, drivers will be delayed 12 billion hours a year.

___ d. Transportation delays now cost travelers billions of dollars.

Paragraph 7   Shizuo Torii, a professor at Toho University in Japan, has studied the sense of smell. He studied the effects that odors have on the feelings and behaviors of humans. By measuring the brain waves of people after they smelled a particular odor, Torii found that some odors produced a brain wave pattern that showed the people were calm. Other odors produced a pattern that showed excitement. It was discovered, for example, that lemon and peppermint have an exciting effect; nutmeg and lavender reduce stress; and a mix of rosemary and lemon will improve concentration. Some Japanese corporations are using the results of this research to make the workplace more productive and pleasant.

Which sentence best states the main idea of the paragraph?

___ a. People's brain waves are different when they smell lemon than when they smell rosemary.

___ b. Japanese corporations want to make the workplace more pleasant and efficient.

___ c. Shizuo Torii is a Japanese professor paid by corporations to improve the workplace environment.

___ d. A Japanese researcher has discovered that smells affect people's brain waves.

Paragraph 6 adapted from "Levitating Trains: Hope for Gridlocked Transportation," by Richard A. Uher, *Futurist* 24, no. 5 (September–October, 1990): 28.
Paragraph 7 adapted from "Aromacology: The Psychic Effects of Fragrances," *Futurist* 24, no. 5 (September–October, 1990): 49.

Paragraph 8   In the United States, old people who no longer have an income or who suffer from a loss of physical abilities are often forced to give up living alone. They must leave their homes and depend on someone else to give them a place to live and to take care of their physical needs: they must either live with relatives or live in homes for the aged. This loss of independence is a major problem for the aged.

Which sentence best states the main idea of the paragraph?

___ a. Being unable to live alone is a serious problem for old people in the United States.

___ b. Old people in the United States who are poor or sick cannot live alone.

___ c. Old people who are poor or sick should live with their relatives, not in homes for the aged.

___ d. In the United States, old people who are poor or sick are forced to live in homes for the aged.

Paragraph 9   Not all of the islands in the Caribbean Sea are the tops of a volcanic mountain range that begins under the sea. Some are the tops of older, nonvolcanic mountains, mountains that have been covered in coral. Coral is a hard, rocklike material that is made of the shells of sea animals called coral polyps. When coral polyps are alive, they attach to any base they can find, such as old mountaintops under the sea. When the polyps die, they leave their shells behind as a rocky covering. Then, new polyps attach to this covering. The result is a coral island. Many of the smaller islands in the Caribbean are coral islands.

Which sentence best states the main idea of the paragraph?

___ a. Some of the islands in the Caribbean Sea are the tops of old, underwater volcanoes.

___ b. There are many small islands in the Caribbean Sea.

___ c. Many of the Caribbean islands are the tops of old mountains that are covered with coral.

___ d. Coral is formed by sea animals called coral polyps.

___ e. There are many mountains in the islands of the Caribbean Sea.

Paragraph 8 adapted from *Psychology,* by Robert E. Silverman (New York: Appleton-Century-Crofts, 1971), 823.
Paragraph 9 adapted from *A World View,* by Clyde P. Patton, Arlene C. Rengert, Robert N. Saveland, Kenneth S. Cooper, and Patricia T. Caro (Atlanta, GA: Silver Burdett and Ginn, 1988), 116.

2

Reading Selection 1

Newspaper Article

Before You Begin   1. Have you ever eaten at McDonald's?

Since the 1950s, when the first McDonald's opened, the restaurant has been serving its hamburgers to millions of customers quickly and cheaply. The workers are usually cheerful and speedy, but have you ever given any thought to their working conditions or salaries? The following newspaper story examines the employment situation at McDonald's. Some people say that the restaurant is a good place for young people to get a start; others say that McDonald's pays little and works people too hard.

2. What do you think? Is McDonald's a good place to work? Do you have an opinion based on your own experience?

Read the article and form your own opinion. Your teacher may want you to do Vocabulary from Context exercise 1 on page 32 before you begin.

Is McDonald's Fair?

1   Three months ago, Mariza Castro left Honduras. Today, she is in the United States, and she has a job. Castro works behind the counter at McDonald's. Speed is an important part of her work life. Fast-food counter workers are expected to serve customers in less than a minute. At McDonald's they say, "Work fast or you don't last."

2   Are McDonald's workers lucky to have their jobs? Or are they being exploited? The answer depends on who you talk to.

3   McDonald's does many good things. For example, no other company hires more young people than McDonald's. More than half of its workers are under 20 years old. McDonald's also has a good record of hiring minority workers. Thirteen percent of its workers are black. This is better than any other U.S. company.

4   But the burger house has its critics as well. The pay bothered Edward Rodriguez. He worked for nearly a year at a Los Angeles McDonald's. During that time he got only one 10-cent raise. "I used to joke that working for McDonald's is the closest thing to slave labor in the U.S. today," he says. Today, most McDonald's pay about $5.00 an hour. They hire new workers constantly. The restaurant has no other choice because 70 percent of its workers quit or are fired every year.

5   But McDonald's also gets its share of praise. Its best workers move up quickly. Just talk to 17-year-old Ameer Abdur-Razaaq of Harlem, New York City. "They call me 'Young Crew Chief' around my block," he says. "Where else can I go at my age and be in charge of this many people?" He sees the job as the first step in his career.

6   However, most McDonald's crew members never make it to manager because the job pressure is so intense and the rewards so few. As one worker put it, "They expect a lot and they don't pay you much."

Excerpted from *News for You,* May 16, 1990.

Comprehension

Answer the following questions according to your understanding of the passage. Your teacher may want you to work individually, in small groups, or in pairs. True/False items are indicated by a T / F before a statement. Some questions may have more than one correct answer. Others require an opinion. Choose the answer you like best; be prepared to defend your choices.

1. What type of restaurant is McDonald's? _____

2. Consider the sentence in paragraph 1, "Work fast or you don't last."

   T / F At McDonald's you will be fired if you do not work fast.

3. T / F McDonald's workers come from different countries.

4. What percentage of McDonald's workers are African American? _____

5. How much do most McDonald's workers make an hour? _____

6. T / F Most of McDonald's workers quit or are fired every year.

7. T / F McDonald's hires more old than young workers.

8. Why did Edward Rodriguez say that working at McDonald's is like slave labor? _____

   _____

9. T / F Ameer Abdur-Razaaq is happy to be a crew chief.

Discussion

The following questions are intended to help you form a critical opinion about McDonald's and about this article. Your teacher may want you to work in pairs or small groups as you answer these questions. You may want to take notes to use in writing a short composition on working conditions at McDonald's.

1. Where did the writer get information about McDonald's? Do you think it is accurate? Consider the figures cited in paragraph 4; where would a writer get this sort of information? And what about Ameer Abdur-Razaaq? Do you think the writer talked to many workers like him? On what do you base your answer?

2. Is McDonald's a good place to work? (Would you like to work at McDonald's?) List the advantages and disadvantages based on the reading and your own experience to support your opinion.

Discussion/Composition

Some people say that McDonald's represents what is good about the United States. Do you agree or disagree? Give information from the reading and your own experience to support your opinion.

Vocabulary from Context

Exercise 1

Both the ideas and vocabulary in the exercise below are taken from "Is McDonald's Fair?" Use the context provided to decide on meanings for the italicized words. Write a definition, synonym, or description in the space provided.

1. _____ Critics of McDonald's say that the workers are *exploited* by the restaurant. The workers are often young, uneducated, and either immigrants or minorities who cannot easily get other jobs and therefore have to take whatever work they can find. Some workers claim that McDonald's exploits this situation by making them work long hours with little pay.

2. _____ My son Benjamin says workers are treated no better than *slave labor.* He claims that the bosses act as if they own you, just like in the early days of the United States when rich farmers bought and sold black workers from Africa. Because of this, he refuses to work for McDonald's.

3. _____

4. _____ Dale and his boss did not get along well. The other night, after Dale broke some dishes, the boss said, "That's it! You're *fired!* Take your last paycheck and leave!" But Dale was just as angry as his boss. He shouted back, "Don't worry! I'm leaving! You can't fire me, because I *quit*!"

5. _____ From the time they arrive until quitting time, McDonald's workers work very hard. The restaurant wants to serve every customer in less than one minute, so the job pressure is *intense.* The workers have no time to rest—they run from one thing to the next with no time to relax or think of anything else.

6. _____ Although McDonald's has been criticized, it has also received a lot of *praise.* For example, Ameer Abdur-Razaaq says that he thinks McDonald's is a good company because it gives young people the chance to earn money and learn important job skills.

Exercise 2

This exercise should be done after you have finished reading "Is McDonald's Fair?" The exercise will give you practice deciding on the meaning of unfamiliar words. Give a definition, synonym, or description of each of the words below. The number in parentheses indicates the paragraph in which the word can be found. Your teacher may want you to do these orally or in writing.

1. (1) counter _____

2. (3, 4) hire _____

3. (4) critics _____

Reading Selection 2

 Technical Prose

Before You Begin   Check your impressions of the United States.

1. What percentage of people living in the United States do you think speak English as their native language?

2. Do you think the percentage of native English speakers in the United States has increased or decreased over the last ten years?

3. You may know that, after English, Spanish is the most common native language of U.S. residents. But what would you guess are the next three most common native languages of U.S. residents?

4. How many U.S. residents do you think have the same native language as yours?

Answers to questions like these can be found in reports written by the U.S. Census Bureau, a government office responsible for counting (every ten years) the number of people in the country. The following newspaper article and table are based on information collected by the Census Bureau. Read them to see if your impressions are correct.

USA Today

Language Mirrors Immigration, Provides Key to Nation's Past, Present

1   The number of residents whose native language is not English has risen 34% in the last ten years to approximately 32 million, according to a recent Census Bureau report. Now one in every seven U.S. residents, or about 14% of the total U.S. population, speaks a language other than English at home.

2   According to the Census Bureau report, there are 329 different languages spoken in U.S. homes. The most common language other than English is Spanish. Seventeen million people, more than half of all the residents who speak a language other than English, speak Spanish. That is ten times as many as speak French, the second most common language, used by 5.3%

of those who don't use English at home. The others of the top five most common languages are German, 4.9%; Italian, 4.1%; and Chinese, 3.9%.

3   Almost 90% of those who speak a language other than English at home communicate in one of the 20 most common of these 329 languages. Many of the 309 other languages are used by very small numbers of people in the United States. For example, there are 750 speakers of Papia Mentae, a Portuguese creole* language, and 73 speakers of Woleai-Ulithi, a Micronesian language.

4   The number of speakers of each language shows the changing pattern of immigration to the United States over the last 100 years. Many European languages

are becoming less common, as immigrants who came to the United States during the first half of the 1900s die. In the last ten years, the number of German speakers decreased 4%, to 1.5 million. The number of Italian speakers decreased 20% to 1.3 million. Polish, the fifth most common foreign language ten years ago, dropped to the seventh most common. The number of Yiddish speakers decreased 33.5% to 213,000.

5   Languages of newer immigrants, on the other hand, are becoming more widely used in the United States. The number of Chinese speakers rose 98% to 1.2 million. The number of speakers of Tagalog, the language of the Philippines, rose 87% to nearly

---

*creole: a language formed as a result of speakers of several languages coming together and creating a new language by which to communicate

850,000. The number of people who speak Kru, an African language, rose 169% to 65,800.

6   More than half of those who do not speak English at home live in just three states, California, New York, and Florida. However, there are non-native English speakers in all states. Often, speakers of particular foreign languages live mainly in just a few states. For example, almost half of the United States's 355,150 Arabic speakers live in California, Michigan, and New York. French speakers are concentrated in Maine, New Hampshire, and Louisiana. A majority of the 429,860 Portuguese speakers can be found in Massachusetts, California, and New Jersey.

7   Most people age 5 or older who speak a foreign language at home also speak at least some English. Fifty-six percent, or 17.9 million people say they speak English "very well," and 23% say they speak it "well." With the help of relatives or foreign-language Census forms, 15.2% answer "not well," and 5.8%–or 1.8 million people–say they don't speak English at all.

8   How well immigrants speak English often reflects how long they've been in the United States. For example, two-thirds of Italian speakers say they know English "very well," compared with just 22% of speakers of Miao. Miao is the language of the Hmong, a people from Laos, most of whom immigrated to the United States after 1975.

The 25 Most-Commonly Spoken Languages in the United States after English

Language	Rank	Number of Speakers	Percentage Change from 10 Years Ago	State with Highest Percentage of Speakers
Spanish	1	17,339,172	+ 50.1	New Mexico
French	2	1,702,176	+ 8.3	Maine
German	3	1,547,099	− 3.7	North Dakota
Italian	4	1,308,648	− 19.9	New York
Chinese	5	1,249,213	+ 97.7	Hawaii
Tagalog	6	843,251	+ 86.6	Hawaii
Polish	7	723,483	− 12.4	Illinois
Korean	8	626,478	+127.0	Hawaii
Vietnamese	9	507,069	+149.8	California
Portuguese	10	429,860	+ 19.1	Rhode Island
Japanese	11	427,657	+ 25.0	Hawaii
Greek	12	388,260	− 5.3	Massachusetts
Arabic	13	355,150	+ 56.4	Michigan
Hindi	14	331,484	+155.0	New Jersey
Russian	15	241,798	+ 38.2	New York
Yiddish	16	213,064	− 33.4	New York
Thai/Lao	17	206,266	+131.8	California
Persian	18	201,865	+ 85.2	California
French Creole	19	187,658	+650.6	Florida
Armenian	20	149,694	+ 46.8	California
Navaho	21	148,530	+ 20.8	New Mexico
Hungarian	22	147,902	− 17.5	New Jersey
Hebrew	23	144,292	+ 45.7	New York
Dutch	24	142,684	− 2.3	Utah
Mon-Khmer	25	127,441	+696.5	Rhode Island

Source: Based on data from the U.S. Census Bureau, *USA Today,* and the *New York Times.*

This article is adapted from two articles by Margaret L. Usdansky: "Language Mirrors Immigration, Provides Key to Nation's Past, Present," *USA Today,* April 28, 1993, 11A, and "Census: Languages Not Foreign at Home," *USA Today,* April 28, 1993, 1A. Copyright © 1993, USA TODAY. Reprinted by permission.

Comprehension

Use information from the article and the table to answer the following questions. True/False items are indicated by a T / F preceding a statement.

1. T / F   Thirty-four percent of all U.S. residents do not speak English as their native language.

2. T / F   The number of U.S. residents whose native language is not English increased by about one-third in the last ten years.

3. T / F   About one-third of the people in the United States whose native language is not English are Spanish speakers.

4. T / F   There are fewer U.S. residents who are native speakers of Mon-Khmer than of any other language.

5. T / F   Most of the U.S. residents who don't speak English at home speak one of only twenty other languages.

6. T / F   The Census Bureau only reported information about languages that are spoken by more than 100 residents.

7. Which language had the greatest percentage increase in the last ten years? _____

8. Which language is the second-fastest growing native language in the United States? _____

9. T / F   Ten years ago, the top five languages (after English) were the same ones as the top five now.

10. T / F   There are fewer native speakers of French in the United States now than there were ten years ago.

11. T / F   There are fewer native speakers of Italian in the United States now than there were ten years ago.

12. Why are there fewer speakers of European languages in the United States now than there were fifty years ago?

   _____

   _____

13. More than half of the residents who don't speak English at home live in which three states?

   _____

14. T / F   About half of the U.S. residents who speak Arabic live in Michigan.

15. T / F   About 38 percent of the U.S. residents who speak Russian at home live in New York.

16. T / F   More than three-fourths of U.S. residents whose native language is not English say they speak English "well" or "very well."

17. T / F   In general, the longer immigrants have been in the United States, the better they say they speak English.

18. T / F   The Census Bureau gets information from U.S. residents who do not speak English very well.

19. Why isn't Indonesian one of the languages listed on the chart? _____

_____

20. How many people in the United States speak your native language in their homes? _____

Discussion/Composition

1. Are there languages in this table that you think will not be among the "top 25 languages" ten years from now? What languages might be added to the chart in ten years? For which other languages do you think the number of speakers will increase or decrease?

2. Some people say that a country is weakened when its residents do not speak the same language. Others believe that a multilingual society strengthens a country. What do you think? Give reasons and examples to support your opinion.

3. Should elementary schools in the United States teach children in the language they speak at home? Be sure to support your opinion.

Reading Selections 3A–3C

Popular Social Science

Before You Begin:
Establishing Your
Point of View

The changing family is a popular topic in magazines, newspapers, and social science texts in North America. These readings often begin by discussing popular definitions of the family. Before you read the articles that follow, consider your own beliefs.

1. Throughout history, people around the world have had different ideas of what a family is. List the people in your family. What is your definition of a family?

Before You Begin:
Comparing Your
Point of View
with Others'

The following description is from a special issue of *Life* magazine on the American Family.

> In a recent study on family and family values, Americans were asked for their definition of the family. Only 22 percent thought a family was "a group of people related by blood, marriage or adoption." The definition preferred by 74 percent was much broader. A family, the majority felt, was "a group of people who love and care for one another."

1. According to the preferred definition, check (✓) those groups below that could be a family.

___ people who live together
___ people and their pets
___ neighbors
___ people who belong to the same church

2. Does the definition in the study surprise you? Do you agree or disagree with it?

The following reading selections discuss families and relationships. Your teacher may want you to do the Vocabulary from Context exercise on pages 39 and 41 before you begin.

Selection 3A   **Trade Book**

Trade books are written on popular topics and are intended for a general audience. Although they sometimes discuss academic topics, these books require no specialized knowledge. The following passages are taken from a trade book called *Families: A Celebration of Diversity, Commitment, and Love.* You will begin by developing a first impression of this book.

From *Life* (Collector's Edition: The American Family), 1992, 4.

Critical Reading

When evaluating a passage, readers often develop a first impression of the point of view of the author and compare it with their own. *Families: A Celebration of Diversity, Commitment, and Love* was written for children about other children's lives so they could see many kinds of human families. Below is a paragraph from the acknowledgments, written by the woman who collected these children's stories. Read it to get your first impression of her.

> Many thanks are due to . . . my own family, for what I have learned from them: my parents, my brother and niece, my ex-husband and his family, my ex-and-thankfully-forever mother-in-law, my children and stepchildren and their spouses, my partner and his family, and, not least, my dearest friends.

1. What is your first impression of the writer?

2. What is your impression of her family?

3. Do you think you will mostly agree or disagree with this writer?

On page 40 is the Introduction to the book. It contains a number of statements about families, some of which you may agree with and others perhaps not. After each paragraph, decide which ideas you agree with and which you disagree with. Underline those with which you agree; circle those with which you disagree. Your teacher may want you to compare your reactions with those of your classmates.

Vocabulary from Context

The vocabulary in the exercise below is taken from various sections of *Families: A Celebration of Diversity, Commitment, and Love* that you will be reading. Use the context provided to decide on meanings for the italicized words. Write a definition, synonym, or description in the space provided.

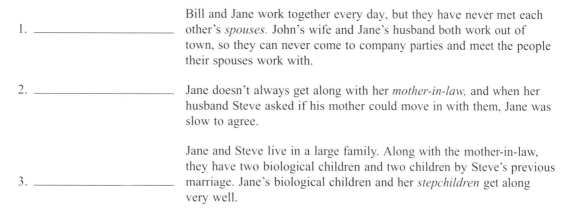

1. _____ Bill and Jane work together every day, but they have never met each other's *spouses.* John's wife and Jane's husband both work out of town, so they can never come to company parties and meet the people their spouses work with.

2. _____ Jane doesn't always get along with her *mother-in-law,* and when her husband Steve asked if his mother could move in with them, Jane was slow to agree.

3. _____ Jane and Steve live in a large family. Along with the mother-in-law, they have two biological children and two children by Steve's previous marriage. Jane's biological children and her *stepchildren* get along very well.

Introduction

Families — what are they? Your family is the people who take care of you, who care about you. Your family may be the person who adopted you. Your family may be your birth mother or father. Your family may include people who joined you, like stepparents and stepbrothers and stepsisters. Your family may be your grandparents, your aunt or uncle, or your guardian. Some kids are able to ask friends to act as family for them — sometimes temporarily — and this can be a big help.

Families change over time. This can be painful, if you miss someone who's moved out of your life. In other ways, it's fine. At different times in your life, when you will have new needs and interests, you may find new people to call on.

Families are spread out over space. Members may move all over the world. You may be able to write to, or telephone, or visit, relatives who live in different kinds of places. It can be a big network you have, a way of learning about places far from your hometown.

Some people think a family is supposed to be a mom and a dad and their children. This can cause a lot of hurt feelings. In school, you may be asked to make a Mother's Day card; but lots of kids don't live with their mothers. You may be asked to bring your dad to work on the school playground for a day; but lots of kids don't live with their dads. Most kids know that, really, families are often very different from "Mom 'n' Dad".

And that "very different" can be a fine thing. A family of two can be close and cozy. A big family can mean there are many people to go to for help or for fun. A family that changes over time means there are different people to be with over your life. A family whose members are very different from each other means you can learn a wide variety of things.

What do *you* think a family is?

Here are some kids' answers to the question.

Excerpts from *Families: A Celebration of Diversity, Commitment, and Love,* by Aylette Jenness (Boston: Houghton Mifflin, 1990), 8, 22–23, 30–31, 32–33, 42, 46–47.

4. _____ Although I do not know them well, I have the *impression* that Jane and Steve are very happy.

5. _____
6. _____ Bill and his wife Sally were not able to have children. Recently, they decided to *adopt* a child whose parents had been killed in an accident. They could have become only the child's *guardians,* but they wanted to do more than take care of her. They wanted her to be legally their daughter, to be part of their family.

7. _____ Jane's brother Paul is *gay.* He and his lover John live very near Jane and Steve and see them often for dinner. Although Paul and John are
8. _____ not legally married, the men have made a lifetime *commitment* to stay together.

9. _____ Today in North America there is a great *diversity* in the kinds of families that people live in. Of course, some people live in traditional families—with husbands or wives and biological children. But others live in a variety of situations—with in-laws and stepchildren, with gay partners and adopted children, with friends and religious groups.

10. _____ When Jane wrote the *acknowledgment* in the beginning of her book, she thanked all the members of her large extended family.

 Selection 3B   **Trade Book**

Following are four descriptions from *Families: A Celebration of Diversity, Commitment, and Love.* For each description think about the following questions.

1. In what ways is this a traditional family?

2. In what ways is it untraditional?

3. By your definition, do you consider that the child lives in a "family"?

4. What special problems does this child face?

5. What are some good aspects of this kind of family?

Your teacher may want you to answer these questions individually, in pairs, or in groups. Your teacher may suggest that you discuss these after each description or wait until you have read them all.

Discussion/Composition

Consider your answers to questions 1–5, above. What are similarities and differences among the families? Which of these four families would you want to live in? Why?

Jaime

Jaime's father came to the United States from Mexico twelve years ago. At first he stayed with his uncle, and worked on a farm. There he began to learn English, and later he moved to California. Jaime's mother came from Mexico a little later, living with her brother until she met and married Jaime's father.

Now they have five sons — Jaime, Salvador, Javier, Gabriel, and Hector. Jaime and Salvador go to school, and Javier goes to a nursery school where both of his parents help the teacher each week. Gabriel and Hector are at home with their mother, where she is busy all the time, washing clothes, cooking, and cleaning for her big family.

Jaime's father has two jobs — he works full time in a restaurant, and part time as a janitor. He says, smiling, "Five kids — I've got to work a lot!"

A few months ago Jaime's whole family went back to Mexico for the first time to visit relatives. Jaime's father says, "I drove nearly fifty hours — two nights and three days." The boys got to know many family members they had never met, especially their grandparents.

Here in the United States, Jaime's family members speak Spanish to each other and to their Mexican-American friends. They speak English to people who can't understand Spanish. Jaime's father wants the boys to do well in school here. He says, "Some people like to get money, and that's it. I don't like that.

School is important. Maybe the boys will have a job like a mailman — or, why not, maybe a doctor or a lawyer."

Jaime likes his school, especially math class and using the computers. After school, he plays with his brothers. Sometimes he helps take care of his littlest brother, Hector. "I pick him up, give him toys, play games with him. Sometimes I help my mother — I clean my room. Sometimes I *don't* help my mother."

"I like playing with my friends — hand wrestling, tag, hide and seek, and soccer." Jaime is on a soccer team, and he practices twice a week after school.

What does he want to be when he grows up? He smiles at his father and says, "I want to be a lawyer."

Elliott

Elliott's family is his two fathers — his "Papa," Dmitri, and his "Daddy," Tom. Dmitri says, "Families come in all shapes and sizes. We happen to be gay men, two men who love each other, but we do the same things that other families do — we make oatmeal for Elliott, we give him baths."

"Dmitri and I knew when we first got together nine years ago that we wanted to be parents," Tom explains. "We started to prepare for a family long before Elliott was born. That's why we bought our house."

"Elliott was adopted at birth," Dmitri says. "His birth mother wasn't able to raise him. Elliott knows her. He sees her from time to time, and he'll be able to ask her questions when he wants to. He'll always have a relationship with her.

"We were in the hospital when Elliott was born, and we brought him home, here, from the hospital. I think that our way of being open about our family helped people accept us. We'd be out pushing the baby carriage in our neighborhood, and neighbors would say, 'Oh, you've got a baby? Congratulations!' We try to make ourselves approachable, so people can ask us questions if they want to.

"We've split up taking care of Elliott pretty evenly," Dmitri continues. "If he gets hurt, he'll run to one of us, say me — I'll pick him up, and then he'll turn to Tom." Dmitri goes to work very early each morning, so Tom helps Elliott get dressed and takes him to his day-care center.

"I like my teachers," Elliott says. "I like it when we read stories in school, and I like drawing and tracing and coloring." Dmitri picks Elliott up and spends the afternoon with him.

"After school I play with my Lego farm," says Elliott. "I paint at my easel. I have a smock. And I like to play Sesame Street on the computer. I can put in the disk. Then I push ENTER. I can make numbers and animals on the computer. I can spell my name, E-L-L-I-O-T-T. You have to be careful. You never shake the computer!"

When Tom comes home, he cooks Elliott's dinner and puts him to bed. "And every night, we sing 'Goodnight, Sweetheart,' " Dmitri says. "Together.

"You know," Dmitri goes on, "I'd like to have six kids. I came from a family of four kids, and I love my siblings. I want Elliott to have that, too. The most I've gotten Tom to commit to is four; I may

have to come down a little. Maybe five."

Tom and Dmitri have begun to make it known that they're available to adopt another child who needs a family. "I want a baby brother!" says Elliott.

Right now they're looking for a bigger house with a bigger yard. Big enough for their three dogs. And — who knows — maybe five kids.

Dmitri says. "We're really not so different from other families. Sometimes adults have more preconceived notions than kids do. The other day I was picking up Elliott at school, and a little girl came up to me. She said, 'Are you Elliott's daddy?' I said, 'Yes.' She said, 'Then who's Tom?' I said, 'He's Elliott's daddy, too.' 'Oh,' she said. Then, almost to herself, 'Elliott's got two daddies. I haven't got any!' "

Eve

"**I** mostly live with my mom," Eve says, "but about two nights a week I go to my dad and my stepmom's house, and I live there and I go to school from there. I have my own room in each house, and in both houses I have desks where I can do my homework.

"I have two brothers, but they're both away at school. And I have a dog, Lion.

"In Dad's house, it's Dad's way, and in Mom's house, it's Mom's way. I've realized that they're different parents, and I shouldn't treat them the same. But sometimes it gets into problems for myself. If I like rules from one house better than the other, I feel like saying, 'I

like it better when you do it *this* way.' But I try to work it out. I usually say, 'Well, I know this is your rules, but I wonder if you would rewrite the rules a little, because I'm disagreeing with some of them.'

"My mom pushes me a lot in my homework, and it helps, 'cause she really makes me do it. At my dad's it's a little bit like, 'Okay, let's do this together.' At my mom's there's more expected of me, and at my dad's there's more done for me. Those are very different, but they're a nice contrast. I like them both.

"When my dad first got married, it was a little hard, because I thought I was expected to treat my stepmother like Mom, but then I realized I didn't have to. I love them both, but I know more about my mom; I know what's going to happen

more. With my stepmom, I have to think a little more, or ask a little more, because she's a lot newer in my life. My mom likes my stepmother, and how she treats me, and my stepmother respects my mom. I consider myself real lucky."

Jennifer

Jennifer lives with her mother and her sister, Merryn, in a commune — a household of people who have chosen to share a home. Her family includes two other small families right now — and Tiger Lily, her cat. Here Jen and Merryn are sitting on the floor in their living room, with their mother behind Merryn.

"I've lived here in this house since I was three. It's always seemed right to me. I love it. I'd be lonelier if it was just my mom and Merryn and me. In this house you make more friends, you meet more people. Of course, it's hard when people leave — they're family, they really *are* family — and you get really close to them. There's a list of about fifty people who've lived here. They come back to visit.

"We have a hard time trying to find new people to move in, 'cause we have to get to know them, we have to see if they can fit into our family style. And everyone has to agree on someone. And of course, *they* have to like it, too."

Family members share housework, help each other in a variety of ways, and spend a lot of time together. "They help me with schoolwork — Jerry's good at math — and they give me rides. We go shopping together, or to the movies. And I'll do favors for them — I baby-sit for Sam, I help them out.

"I love my family. I can't imagine living anywhere else."

Selection 3C   **Trade Book**

On pages 50–51 is the Postscript from the book *Families: A Celebration of Diversity, Commitment, and Love.* Read it quickly, then return to the Discussion and Discussion/Composition questions on this page.

Discussion

1. Why do you think the author chose to do an exhibit on the topic of families? Why do you think she decided to use parts of the exhibit to write a book about children for children?

2. Peoples' definitions of a family can change over time and can be different depending on where they live. Do you think this book would be popular around the world? Do you think this book could have been written 50 years ago?

Discussion/Composition

1. Pretend you are a reviewer for a newspaper in your community. Write a review of this book based on the parts you have read. Be sure to describe the book and then to evaluate it.

2. The Postscript includes 4 pictures and 7 written comments by visitors to the exhibit. Notice that some of the comments have responses. Write a response to one of the comments or pictures. You may agree or disagree with the point of view, or you may try to be helpful or kind to the person.

Postscript

This book began as a photographic exhibition at The Children's Museum in Boston, Massachusetts. Many families joined the project, allowing me to photograph and interview them, generously sharing their feelings and ideas. Kids spoke of their problems, pleasures, interests, and hopes, and carefully corrected and approved my edited versions of their taped conversations.

In the finished exhibit, a table with paper, crayons, and pencils encouraged visitors to join the show. Kids made drawings and stories about their own families and put them up on the walls. Many were joyous: "I have a family and they love me; that's the way it's going to be." Others expressed the pain of family problems in pictures and words: "I wish I had a nice family. If your parents are divorced, be thankful!"

Adults wrote about their own experiences and opinions, and posted these:

"I've been part of a big family, a single-parent (me) family, and a traditional family. I think it's all the same! . . . I think that if you love someone you have to work at it. That can relate to 1 other person or 100 other people. And we are all in the *human* family."

"Families are precious! The diversity here makes me realize the strength, the willingness and bondedness that hold us together. To be unique, irreplaceable and unrepeatable, that is family. Color, size, denomination or preferences only add flavor and texture to a beautiful commodity."

One visitor asked, "I have only one question. Is it wrong to be idealistic and want a traditional family with a mom and dad, a couple of kids, a dog and a cat, and grandparents who live in St. Louis?"

And another replied, "No. This exhibit makes no judgment in regard to right and wrong. It acknowledges that there are many kinds of families in addition to the traditional one."

One teenager found help: "When I first found out about my daddy being gay I was very upset, but after seeing what you have about being gay I feel a lot better about his sexual preferences. Thank you sooo much."

And many people voiced this sentiment: "The photographs show that the traditional family unit is changing; however, this transition is preserving the only really important ingredient to make a family — love."

Reading Selection 4
Technical Prose

The families you have just read about show changing lifestyle patterns in the United States. Below is a statistical discussion of changes in marriage patterns. It is based on a U.S. Census Bureau* report.

Overview

Read the first two paragraphs of "Marriage Taking a Back Seat, Says Census" to get a general idea of its content. Indicate if each statement below is true (T) or false (F) according to your understanding of these paragraphs.

1. T / F   The average age of marriage for both men and women is higher now than it was 20 years ago.

2. T / F   More people are living together without being married today than did 20 years ago.

3. T / F   Most young people today will never marry.

4. T / F   Most children in the United States live with only one parent.

Now, look at the full article to answer the Comprehension questions on page 53. Your teacher may want you to do the Vocabulary from Context exercise on page 54 before you begin.

Marriage Taking a Back Seat, Says Census

UNITED PRESS INTERNATIONAL

1 WASHINGTON—Men and women are waiting longer than ever to marry, a Census Bureau report said yesterday, and the number of unmarried couples living together has more than quadrupled in the past 20 years.

2 At the same time, the report said the number of children affected by divorce, separation, and out-of-wedlock births continues to rise and fewer than three-quarters of all children now live with both parents.

3 According to the report, an examination of marital status and living arrangements showed that the median age for a man's first marriage is 26.2 years, breaking the previous high of 26.1 years set in 1890.

The median age for a woman's first marriage is 23.8, higher than any previously recorded level.

4 "At the beginning of the 20th century, the median age at first marriage started a decline that ended in the mid-1950's," the report said, "reaching a low in 1956 of 20.1 years for women and 22.5 years for men."

5 Delays in marriage are also reflected by increases in the proportion of men and women who have not yet married for the first time.

6 The proportion of men and women in their 20s and early 30s who have never married grew substantially.

7 In the last 20 years, "the proportion never married at ages 20 to 24 increased by 75 percent for women and 41 percent for men," the report said.

8 "The proportion for those in the 25–29 age group tripled for women and more than doubled for men. For those in the 30–34 age group, the never-married proportions tripled for both men and women."

9 At the same time, the report

Adapted from "Marriage Taking a Back Seat," *Seattle Post-Intelligencer,* July 12, 1990, A16.
*The U.S. Census Bureau takes a population count every ten years. Census questionnaires provide a variety of information about people living in the United States.

showed that the number of unmarried-couple households continued to rise, from 523,000 20 years ago to 2.8 million today.

10   The majority of partners in unmarried-couple relationships— 59 percent—had never been married, while 32 percent were divorced, 4 percent widowed and 5 percent were separated from their spouses.

11   "The typical age of the partners was 25 to 34 years, 27 percent were under age 25, and 17 percent were age 35 to 44," the report said.

12   "In 6 of 10 unmarried households, both partners were under 35 years of age."

13   The proportion of children under 18 years living with two parents has declined considerably

as divorce, separation, and births to unmarried mothers have become more common.

14   In the past 20 years, the proportion living with two parents declined while the proportion living with one parent doubled from 12 percent to 24 percent, the report said.

Comprehension

Indicate if each statement below is true (T) or false (F) according to your understanding of the article.

1. T / F   Six times as many unmarried couples are living together today as did 20 years ago.

2. T / F   Today, three-quarters of all children are affected by divorce.

3. T / F   The oldest average age for men marrying was recorded in 1890.

4. T / F   The youngest average age at which men and women married was recorded in 1956.

5. T / F   Over the past 20 years, the proportion of people who have never married increased by 75 percent for women and 41 percent for men.

6. T / F   The increase in the proportion of people who have never married has been greater for younger people than for older people.

7. T / F   Most people living in unmarried-couple relationships are divorced.

8. T / F   Most people living in unmarried-couple relationships are between 25 and 34 years of age.

Critical Reading

Why do you think the article refers to people who have never married as "waiting longer to marry" (paragraph 1) and people "who have not yet married for the first time" (paragraph 5)? Do you think this is a good choice of words?

Discussion/Composition

1. List three reasons why a person might choose not to marry. Why are some people concerned about others not marrying—Religious reasons? Worries about the care of children? Concern that old people won't be taken care of? Can you think of other reasons? Are these causes of concern for you?

2. What are the effects on children of changing family patterns? Are new freedoms that encourage more diversity in families helpful or harmful to children? Use examples from your reading and personal experience.

3. When the results of a study are only briefly reported, it is sometimes necessary to use your general knowledge to try to interpret the results. This article reports that people in the United States began to marry at a younger age at the beginning of the 20th century; then the average age for marriage began to rise in the mid-1950s. Why do you think the marriage age declined? Why do you think it rose again?

Vocabulary from Context

The vocabulary in the exercise below is taken from "Marriage Taking a Back Seat, Says Census." Use the context provided to decide on meanings for the italicized words. Write a definition, synonym, or description in the space provided.

1. _____
2. _____

When Sally and Tom got married, people thought they were the perfect couple. But things didn't work out. First they tried a *separation.* Living apart made them realize that they should never have gotten married. In May, their marriage ended in *divorce.*

3. _____
4. _____

5. _____

6. _____

When Jesse and Rachel got married, they knew they wanted to live in a traditional *nuclear family*—mother, father, and biological children. Each of them had come from other family *arrangements,* and they had decided that a more traditional arrangement was what they wanted. Rachel had been born *out of wedlock.* Because her parents had never married, she had never met her biological father. Jesse's mother had been *widowed.* His father's early death made Jesse want to have a large family.

7. _____

When Doris and Henry decided to get married, their friends were surprised. Doris and Henry were only 20 years old, and their friends expected that the couple would *delay* marriage at least until they finished college.

8. _____

At the beginning of the 20th century the average age at which people married began to *decline.* There are a number of reasons why people began to get married earlier, many of which are related to industrialization.

9. _____

Sue doesn't see why anyone else should care whether or not she is married. When strangers ask her whether she is married, she tells them that her marital *status* is none of their business.

10. _____

The *proportion* of people who never marry has been increasing. Many people, including gay men and lesbians, no longer feel that they must marry.

Reading Selection 5

 ## Literature

The following selection is adapted from *Silas Marner,* a famous nineteenth-century English novel by George Eliot. Marner is a weaver, a person who makes cloth from cotton or wool on a large machine called a loom. He lives alone and works day and night without thought of rest or friends. He just sits at his loom and weaves cloth for the people of Raveloe. Because he has no family, he spends all of his time thinking about his money, which he collects in a metal pot hidden under his floor. He is lonely and thinks only about his money, but he is not completely without feeling.

As you read this selection, decide what you think of Silas Marner.

—Do you think you would like Silas Marner?

—Do you know anyone who is like him? Can you understand the way he acts?

Read the selection through completely without stopping to look up unfamiliar words. Your teacher may want you to do the Vocabulary from Context exercise on pages 57–59 before you begin.

Excerpt from Silas Marner
George Eliot

1   Year followed year, and still Silas lived alone. The gold coins rose in the metal pot. He watched them and he worked. That was his life. No other thought, no other person had any part in it. The loom curved his back and his arms and legs, so that when he left it, the curves remained. It also gave his eyes a strange look. He was not forty years old, but his face was dry and yellow like an old man's. The children always called him "Old Master Marner."

2   But love was not quite dead in his heart. Every day he had to bring water from a well and for this purpose he bought a small brown pot. Indeed, it was one of the few things for which he had taken money from his metal pot. The pot was his most prized possession. He took pleasure in the touch of its round, smooth surface and firm handle as much as he enjoyed the satisfaction of having the cool, clear water ready for use. It had been his friend for twelve years, always standing in the same spot, always waiting for him to go to the well in the morning. Then one day, as he was returning from the well, he dropped it and it broke into three pieces. He picked up the pieces with a broken heart and stuck them together. Even though the pot would be of no use, he set it in its spot as a memorial for a lost friendship.

3   This is the history of Silas Marner until the fifteenth year after he came to Raveloe. The whole day he spent at his loom, his ears filled with the boring click of his weaving, his eyes bent close down on the threads, his arms and legs moving

Adapted from *Silas Marner,* by George Eliot (New York: Dodd, Mead, and Co., 1948), 25–27.

thoughtlessly in the same motions. But at night came his celebration. He closed and locked the door, shuttered the windows, and took out his gold. Long ago the pile of coins had become too large for the iron pot and he had made two thick leather bags. Out poured the gold and silver pieces! How bright they shined! There was more gold than silver, and he spent the shillings and other small silver coins on his few necessities. His favorites were the gold pounds, but he loved them all. He spread them out in piles and bathed his hands in them; then he counted them and set them up in regular columns, and felt their rounded outline between his thumb and fingers, and thought fondly of the gold that was only half earned in his loom. "These are not all," he thought. "Others are on the way, like children not yet born. Year will follow year and still they will come."

4   But about Christmas of that fifteenth year a great change came over Marner's life, and his history became part of the histories of his neighbors.

Comprehension

Answer the following questions according to your understanding of the passage. Your teacher may want you to work individually, in small groups, or in pairs. True/False items are indicated by a T / F before a statement. Some questions may have more than one correct answer. Others require an opinion. Choose the answer you like best; be prepared to defend your choices.

1. T / F   Silas had a large circle of family and friends.

2. Why was the loom so important in Silas's life? _____

_____

3. How old was Silas at this point in the story? How did he look? _____

_____

4. How long had he lived in Raveloe? _____

5. What does the brown pot tell us about Silas Marner? (Check all that are correct.)

___ a. He spends very little money on his comforts.
___ b. He has no running water in the house.
___ c. He is a skilled potter.
___ d. He appreciates beauty.
___ e. He keeps only tools that are useful.
___ f. He is capable of love.

6. T / F   A shilling is worth more than a pound.

7. Silas compares his coins to children. What does this tell us about him? (Check all that are correct.)

    — a. He is lonely.
    — b. He has come to love his coins as if they were his family.
    — c. He does not need people to be happy.
    — d. He is an honest man.

8. What does the author mean in paragraph 3 by "he bathed his hands" in the money? _____

_____

9. a. Draw a picture of a pile of coins.

    b. Now draw a picture of a column of coins.

Discussion

1. This selection is part of a novel. Do you think it occurs at the beginning, middle, or end of the novel? Explain your answer.

2. In paragraph 4, it says that Marner's "history became part of the histories of his neighbors." What do you think this means? What "great change" do you think will happen in Marner's life?

Discussion/Composition

Write a paragraph to begin the next chapter in *Silas Marner.* Use the ideas and the vocabulary from this selection. In your paragraph give some idea about the change that you think will occur in Marner's life.

Vocabulary from Context

Both the ideas and the vocabulary in the exercise below are taken from the excerpt from *Silas Marner.* Use the context provided to decide on meanings for the italicized words. Write a definition, synonym, or description in the space provided.

1. _____   Silas Marner lived by himself and spent all of his time working, caring for nothing but making money. In the evening, after he had collected payment for his cloth, he would sit by candlelight and count the piles of *pounds and shillings* that he earned for his work.

2. _____

3. _____

The *loom* where he worked stood in the corner by the fireplace. Apart from the table and one chair it was the only piece of furniture in his house, and he spent most of the hours of his life seated at it, *weaving* cloth for the women of Raveloe.

4. _____

Marner did not own much—the clothes he wore every day, some pots and pans for cooking, the loom. But he did have one *possession* that was very important to him: the brown pot that he used to carry water from the well.

5. _____

You could say that Marner was a sad and unhappy person, a man without *pleasures,* even simple ones such as walks in the forest, or reading, or listening to music. Unlike most people, he did not do things for enjoyment.

6. _____

There was only one thing that made him happy, and this was collecting and saving money. This one *satisfaction* was the only pleasure he allowed himself, and as the years passed he became more and more focused on this task.

7. _____

He had no use for religion and, if anyone had asked, he would have said that he had no use for anything or anyone. But when his little brown pot broke, he put it back together and placed it on the shelf, like a *memorial* to the twelve years that it had served him. Like the stones in the cemetery that marked the final resting place of the dead, the broken pot reminded him of something he had loved.

8. _____

Most people would consider Marner's life to be *boring;* it never changed from day to day, and nothing happened to bring him happiness or excitement.

9. _____

As he worked at his loom, all that could be heard was the small *click* of the pieces of the machine as they hit against each other. No other sound in the silence: *click, click, click* as he worked throughout the day and into the night.

10. _____

He was, of course, a very good weaver. This was to be expected, since he did nothing else all day long. In his hands the cotton and wool *threads* became, as if by magic, whole pieces of cloth that the women of Raveloe would make into shirts or dresses for their families.

11. _____

Marner observed no holidays. Not Christmas, nor birthdays, nor any other *celebration.* He took no time away from his work for such enjoyment.

12. _____

But he did have one special celebration: the counting of his money. At night, when he was finished working for the day, and just before he went to bed, he would close the house up tight so that no one would see him. He would shut the door and *shutter* the window, and pull his money from its hiding place to count it.

13. _____

He would pour the money out on the table and run his fingers through the gold and silver coins. He would count every pound and shilling, and stack the money into little *columns* that stood like the buildings of a small city in front of him.

14. _____

Marner had no other possessions, no family, no friends, no one to love. But he was as *fond of* his money as any of the villagers were of their children.

3

Nonprose Reading

Campus Map

When you make your first visit to a college or university in North America, you will usually be given a map of the campus. Sometimes the map will also include other useful information. On pages 62–64 you will find information that originally appeared with a map of the University of British Columbia (UBC), located in Vancouver, British Columbia. Founded in 1915, UBC provides instruction, research, and public service. As you can see, the university offers a wide variety of activities, programs, and services. The map itself is at the back of the book.

Answer the following questions about UBC. Your teacher may want you to work individually, in pairs, or in small groups. True/False items are indicated by a T / F before a statement. Some questions may have more than one correct answer. Others require an opinion. Choose the answer you like best; be prepared to defend your choices.

Part 1

Pages 62–64 provide a list of places to go and things to do. Refer to these pages as you answer questions 1–4.

1. Under how many sections is the information listed? _____

2. Under which section would you expect to find the libraries and bookstores listed? _____

3. Under which section would you look to find information about something to eat?_____

4. Circle the places that interest you the most.

Part 2

Notice the letters and numbers to the left of each listing. This refers to the location on the map where each place can be found. For example, under "More Literate," the listing for the UBC library shows it is located in section D3 on the map. Use the map and the listings to answer the following questions.

5. Circle the main library on the map; how far is it from the bookstore? _____

6. Does the University have tennis courts? _____

7. a. What road takes you from the library to the Tennis Bubble? _____

    b. Would you take a bus between the two? _____

    c. If you get hurt playing tennis, where could you get medical attention on campus? _____

    _____

8. After getting help at the University Hospital, you decide to get something to eat. What is the closest place with food? What phone number would you call to get more information?

    _____

9. Can you take a bus from the University Hospital to the Botanical Gardens? _____

10. Find the Old Barn Coffee Shop on the map. Can you drive to it from the main library? _____

11. If you need the telephone number of a campus office, what number would you call? _____

12. a. What number should you call if you want to know the telephone number of an office on

    campus? _____

    b. What would *you* do on Saturday if you needed to know a number? _____

    _____

BETTER PREPARED

Executive Programmes (Angus Bldg.)
D3
Seminars and workshops to help executives and
professionals maintain and upgrade management skills.
Courses in marketing, human resources, finance, strategic
planning, personal communications and management.
Catalogue. 822-8400.

Extra-Sessional Studies
A3
Winter and Term I summer evenings, Term II summer
day-time courses, plus directed studies abroad. Course fees
are the same as winter session. Calendar. 822-2657.

Centre for Continuing Education
B1
Courses in the arts, humanities, sciences, personal and career
development, communications, languages and travel. All
programs are non-credit; most have no prerequisites. Classes
on campus, year-round. Calendar. 222-2181.

UBC Women's Resources Centre
Career and personal counselling services for women and
men. Vocational testing, job-search skills, assertiveness
training and building self-esteem. Year-round. Located at
#1–1144 Robson St., Vancouver. 685-3934

UBC Access (Library Processing Centre)
F2
Guided independent study. Degree-credit courses in
agricultural sciences, arts, education, forestry and post-RN
nursing. Information throughout B.C., 8:30 a.m.–4:30 p.m.
Long distance, call collect. 822-6565.

Distance Education–Faculty of Education (Scarfe Bldg.)
E4
Continuing education opportunities for practicing B.C.
teachers through: off-campus direct instruction courses;
video study and Knowledge Network courses; summer
institute courses; and special projects. Credit and non-credit.
822-2013.

MORE LITERATE

UBC Library
D3
Second-largest library in Canada, 17 branches, 2.9 million books,
journals, newspapers, maps, microforms, government
publications, classical records, taped books for the blind and
more. Open to all. Cards $50 per year, $10 per year for seniors.
822-2077. ♿ Partial

UBC Bookstore
E3
Excellent selection of over 70,000 titles, including children's and
general-interest material; UBC souvenirs, stationery, computers
and more. Weekdays 8:30 a.m.to 5:00 p.m.; Wednesday until 8:30
p.m.; Saturday 9:30 a.m.–5:00 p.m. 822-2665. ♿

University of British Columbia Press (Old Auditorium)
C4
Second-largest scholarly press in Canada. Published works
include the Atlas of British Columbia, popular Canadian
biography and history, Pacific Rim studies and more. Authors
include UBC faculty, international scholars and lay authors.
Catalogue. 822-5959.

MORE WORLDLY

International House
C4
Student centre with services and programs for both international
and Canadian students. Services for international students
include reception, orientation, housing and resource information,
and year-round educational, cultural and social activities.
822-5021.

Asian Centre
C4
Special events and programs to increase understanding and
awareness of Asia. The Asian library is Canada's national
repository for Japanese government publications. Facilities may
be rented for public events with an Asian theme. 822-2746. ♿

THOROUGHLY ENTERTAINED

UBC School of Music
C4
Memorable performances by students, faculty and special guests.
Series' run September through March, with a major opera
performed in the spring; summer concerts in July and August.
Free admission to most concerts. 822-3113. ♿ Passable

Frederic Wood Theatre
C4
Training ground for some of Canada's award-winning theatre
people. Four plays per season in the 400-seat proscenium theatre.
Evening performances during winter and summer sessions.
Subscription package available. 822-3880.

Fine Arts Gallery (Main Library)
D3
Mounts exhibitions of contemporary art on a regular basis.
Programs include lecture series, publications and special events.
822-2759. ♿ Passable

MORE RELAXED

UBC Botanical Garden
J5
A 70-acre living museum features plants from all the temperate
regions of the world. 822-4208. The Shop in the Garden has a
wide range of books and garden gifts. 822-4529. ♿ Passable

University of British Columbia Campus Map

C5 | **Nitobe Memorial Garden**
Considered one of the finest Japanese gardens outside Japan. Near the Museum of Anthropology. 822-6038. Season passes and group rates for all gardens. Free admission Wednesdays.

E4 | **Neville Scarfe Children's Garden**
West Coast forest grotto, clover meadow, stream, pond, vegetable and flower gardens which appeal to daycare, pre-school and school groups. Visitors welcome anytime. 822-3767. ♿

MORE AWARE

F4 | **M.Y. Williams Geological Museum**
4.5 billion years of mineral and fossil treasures, including the mineral collection and the incredible 80-million-year-old Lambeosaurus dinosaur. Year-round, weekdays, 8:30 a.m.–4:30 p.m. Free. Collector Shop, Wednesdays 1:30–4:30 p.m. 822-5586. ♿

B4 | **UBC Museum of Anthropology**
Stunning display of Northwest Coast Indian art, including Bill Reid's massive sculpture "Raven and the First Men;" outstanding 15th- to 19th-century European ceramics collection; award-winning building of soaring glass and concrete, overlooking mountains and sea. Guided tours for groups. Gift shop. Admission charge. Tuesday 11:00 a.m. to 9:00 p.m.; Wednesday to Sunday 11:00 a.m. to 5:00 p.m. Closed Mondays. 822-3825. ♿

GROWN WISER

UBC Research Farm
Self-supporting, 700-hectare dairy, forage and forestry research facility. Weekday tours; salmon rearing and spawning channel and small hatchery; open house in July. Free. Oyster River, Vancouver Island. 923-4219. ♿ Partial

Malcolm Knapp Research Forest
32 kilometres of foot trails over a 5,150-hectare research forest. Deer and other wildlife frequently sighted by visitors. Free. About 60 kilometres east of UBC, north of Haney, along 232nd St. to end of Silver Valley Rd., Maple Ridge. 463-8148. ♿

Alex Fraser Research Forest
This 9,000-hectare forest with eight lakes is a great destination for summer camping. Weekdays 8:00 a.m.to 4:30 p.m.; weekends by appointment. Free. Williams Lake, B.C. 392-2207.

IN BETTER SHAPE

H2 | **Thunderbird Winter Sports Centre**
Three ice rinks, a curling rink, two racquetball and four squash courts, a lounge with large sports screen and a private banquet room. Year-round. 822-6121. ♿ Partial

H2 | **Community Sport Services** (Thunderbird Winter Sports Centre)
Year-round programs for the whole family. UBC's summer hockey school draws thousands of young people from around the world. Also gymnastics, fencing, badminton, soccer, cycling, field hockey, golf, sports camp and more. 822-3688.

H2 | **UBC Tennis Centre**
Year-round training facility for adults and juniors. Ten outdoor and four indoor courts. Pro shop and full racquet-stringing service. 822-2505. ♿

D2 | **UBC Aquatic Centre**
More than 300,000 people a year splash down in UBC's two award-winning, olympic-size pools — one indoor, one outdoor. Weightlifting area downstairs. 822-4521. ♿

For information about and results of UBC athletic events, call 222-BIRD.

READY FOR TOMORROW

F4 | **UBC Astronomical Observatory**
Telescopes open for free public viewing most clear Saturdays, year-round, dark to midnight. Always call ahead: 822-6186. Tours, day-time viewing and group observing sessions by appointment: 822-2802.

F4 | **UBC Geophysical Observatory**
Every tremble in Vancouver is recorded on the Lower Mainland's most sensitive earthquake network, displayed here at UBC. Find out about *The Big One*, watch gravity change and more. Guided and self-guided tours. Free. 822-2802. ♿

K1 | **TRIUMF**
World's largest cyclotron, used to study the properties of subatomic particles and to find practical uses for them. Experiments conducted by 400 to 500 scientists each year from 24 countries. Tours. 222-1047. ♿ Partial

K1 | **Dairy Cattle Teaching and Research Centre**
Barn tours bring dairy agriculture to life for school children. For curious adults and agri-professionals, a glimpse of research facilities and technology that are second to none. 822-4593. ♿

MORE SOCIABLE

D4 **UBC Food Services** (Ponderosa)
Many unique locations throughout the campus can accommodate every dining need, from our famous cinnamon buns to gourmet catering. Some locations open for the academic term only. Subway Cafeteria in SUB open year-round. 822-2616. ♿ Subway

A3 **Cecil Green Park**
Book your next reception, meeting or wedding in the rosewood and oak elegance of a bygone era. Panoramic view of English Bay and Howe Sound. Superior catering. 822-6289. ♿

D2 **SUB: Student Union Building**
Hub of student cultural, social and recreational activities and a year-round conference centre with 22 meeting rooms, UN-style board room, movie theatre, bar and pub facilities, plus cafeteria and full catering. 822-2901. Bookings 822-3456/3465. ♿

C1 **UBC Conference Centre** (Gage Residences)
Largest university conference centre in Canada. Available for meetings ranging in size from 10 to several thousand, May through August. Over 500 meeting rooms and accommodation for more than 3,000 people in three residences. 822-5442. ♿

Visitor Accommodation: Inexpensive accommodation for groups and individual visitors year-round. 822-2963.

H2 **The Thunder Deck**
Enjoy your favorite refreshments and food at the south end of the Winter Sports Centre overlooking the playing fields, tennis courts and Georgia Strait. May to September. 822-6121.

MORE IN TOUCH

Campus Telephone Directory Assistance
Monday through Friday, 8:00 a.m. to 4:30 p.m. 822-2211.

C4 **Community Relations Office** (Old Administration Bldg.)
General information on publicly accessible UBC events, programs and facilities. Weekdays, 8:30 a.m. to 4:30 p.m. On campus, look for UBC Reports, a bi-weekly tabloid of campus news and events. 822-3131.

C4 **UBC Speakers Bureau** (Old Administration Bldg.)
You choose the topic, UBC provides the speaker. Faculty and professional staff available to address your club, association, class, conference or business group, September through April. 822-6167.

D2 **Summer Campus Tours** (Student Union Bldg.)
Our gardens, museums and recreational facilities are especially scenic during the summer. Friendly student guides lead free drop-in or pre-booked walking tours. Specialized tours for seniors, children, English-as-a-second-language groups, persons with disabilities and other groups. May through August. 822-3131. ♿

F2 **University Hospital–UBC Site**
One of Vancouver's major hospitals is located right on campus. UBC enjoys a special relationship with this centre as many of UBC's medical faculty teach and practice in this fully equipped hospital. 822-7121. Emergency Service. 822-7222. ♿

C2 **Legal Clinic** (Curtis Bldg.)
Legal services and advice provided by supervised second- and third- year UBC law students for those unable to afford a lawyer. 822-5911. ♿

F1 **Dental Clinic** (MacDonald Bldg.)
Dental services from routine to specialized performed by supervised UBC dentistry students for a reasonable charge. Emergency Clinic runs September to April. 822-2112. ♿ Passable

C2 **School and College Liaison Office** (Brock Hall)
Information about undergraduate programs, admission requirements and student services. Free, guided walking tours of campus for prospective students offered most Friday mornings. 822-4319. ♿

E1 **Office of the Registrar** (General Services Administration Bldg.)
Coordinates admissions, registration and graduation for UBC students. Publications available: Admissions Guide; College-University Transfer Guide; and University Calendar. Year-round hours 8:30 a.m. to 4:00 p.m., weekdays. 822-2844. ♿

J5 **Hortline** (Botanical Garden Centre)
Horticulture advice and information. Monday through Wednesday, 12:00 p.m. to 3:30 p.m., May through August. Tuesday and Wednesday, 12:30 p.m. to 3:30 p.m., September through April. 822-5858.

A3 **Alumni Association** (Cecil Green Park)
Links the university with the community through UBC graduates. To participate in any of the association's activities, call 822-3313. ♿

B3 **Development Office** (Mary Bollert Hall)
Works to advance the goals of the university by increasing private funding. Individuals, corporations, foundations and service organizations contribute to UBC's development through annual, special and major campaign gifts. Monies raised are used for buildings, scholarships, endowed chairs, library acquisitions, equipment and other academic projects. 822-8900. ♿ Passable, phone ahead

B4 **Parking and Security**
Manages all on-campus parking as well as patrolling the campus and providing information and security services. 822-4721. ♿

WELL TRAVELLED

Enjoy the breathtaking scenery of beaches, mountains and the University Endowment Lands on your way to UBC. Bicycle racks throughout the campus and large carparks at each of the four corners. 822-4721.

Five major bus routes will get you here. From downtown: No. 4 UBC via 4th Ave., No.10 UBC via Broadway and 10th Ave. From Burnaby: No.25 King Edward, beginning at Brentwood Mall. From South Vancouver: No.41 via 41st Ave. and Southwest Marine Dr.; No.49, from Metrotown Skytrain Station via 49th Ave.

Word Study

Stems and Affixes

Below is a chart showing some commonly occurring stems and affixes.* Study their meanings, then do the exercises that follow. Notice that the stems all refer to common actions. Your teacher may ask you to give examples of other words you know that are derived from these stems and affixes.

Prefixes

de-	away, down, reverse the action of	depart, deport, dehumanize, defrost, desalt
e-, ex-	out, away	export
in-, im-	in, into, on	import, income
pre-	before	prehistoric, prepare
re-, retro-	again, back	replay, return
tele-	far, distant	telephone
trans-	across	trans-Atlantic

Stems

-audi-, -audit-	hear	audience, auditorium
-dic-, -dict-	say, speak	predict
-fact-, -fect-, -fic-	make, do	factory
-graph-, -gram-	write, writing	telegram
-mit-, -miss-	send	emit, missionary
-pon-, -pos-	put, place	position
-port-	carry	transport
-scrib-, -script-	write	manuscript
-spect-	look	spectator, inspect
-vid-, -vis-	see	vision, visit
-voc-, -vok-	call	vocal, revoke

Suffixes

-able, -ible, -ble (adj.)	capable of, fit for	doable, visible
-er, -or (noun)	one who	reader, spectator
-ion, -tion (noun)	state, condition, the act of	description
-ize (verb)	to make, to become	vocalize

---

*For a list of all stems and affixes taught in *Choice Readings, International Edition: Book 1,* see the Appendix.

____

Exercise 1

1. What does *in retrospect* mean in the following sentence?

   In retrospect, I think I made a good decision to study engineering.

   a. looking back   c. speaking honestly

   b. recently   d. surprisingly

2. Use your knowledge of stems and affixes to explain how the following words were formed.

   television _____

   telegram _____

   transportation _____

3. The prefix *pre-* (meaning before) often combines with simple verbs to create new verbs (for example, *pre-* + *view* becomes *preview*). List three words you know that use *pre-* in this way.

   _____

4. *-Sap-*, or *-sag-* is a root that means wise or knowing. It appears in *homo sapiens*, the scientific name for humans. It also appears in *sage*, a wise person. What do you think a *presage* is? Here is a sentence to give you some context clues:

   The dark skies were a *presage* of the coming storm.

   _____

5. *Migrate* means to move from one place to another. Explain the difference between *immigration* and *emigration.*

   _____

6. *Re-*, with the meaning *again*, is a commonly used prefix. Circle the words below in which *re* is a prefix and means again.

repaint	rear	reread	reuse	reborn
ready	reform	religion	remake	real

Exercise 2

Word analysis can help you to guess the meaning of unfamiliar words. Using context clues and what you know about word parts, write a definition, synonym, or description of the italicized words.

1. _____ Maria plans to study *vocal* music at the university.

2. _____ Because he likes to watch television in the kitchen and the bedroom, Steve bought a *portable* TV.

3. _____ We can't hear that radio station here; it can only *transmit* its signal 30 miles.

4. _____ Cameras outside the front door of the bank *videotape* everyone who goes in or out.

5. _____ It is difficult to travel by train when there are very few *porters* to help travelers get their suitcases on and off the train.

6. _____ The director *dictated* a letter into a tape recorder.

7. _____ The photographer used a *telephoto* lens to take a picture of the movie stars swimming at their private pool.

8. _____ The U.S. *imports* many automobiles from other countries.

9. _____ All the teachers have a key for the room where the *audiovisual* equipment is kept.

10. _____ The king *imposed* heavy new taxes on the people of his country to pay for building his new palace.

11. _____ The students damaged the top of the wooden desk by *inscribing* their names on it with a pocket knife.

12. _____ My television was *manufactured* in Korea.

13. _____ Xian had trouble *visualizing* what it would be like to live in a foreign country for four years.

14. _____ The children ran up to the soccer star, holding out pencils and paper and asking for his *autograph*.

15. _____ Good readers make *predictions* about what a passage will say before they read it.

16. _____ We cannot move into the apartment unless we *prepay* three months' rent.

17. _____ Please *remit* your payment to the address shown at the top of your telephone bill.

18. _____ The *emissions* from automobiles make the air unhealthy.

19. _____ There was a crowd of *spectators* at the scene of the accident.

20. _____ According to the *edict* of the *dictator* on December 1, it is illegal to
21. _____ say anything bad about the government.

22. _____ The king was *deposed* by revolutionaries who wanted to control the
government themselves.

23. _____ Looking through my old family photographs *evokes* wonderful
memories of my childhood.

24. _____ The *deforestation* of the world's rain forests is a serious problem.

25. _____ Before each new car leaves the *factory, inspectors* examine it
26. _____ carefully, looking for any problems in how it looks or how it works.

27. _____ The President's speech was *televised* at 8:00 P.M.

28. _____ My uncle *remarried* a year after his first wife died.

29. _____ Oakland University told Jim to *reapply* for admission next year.

30. _____ The pilot asked the ground workers to *de-ice* the wings of the plane
before he tried to take off in the winter storm.

31. _____ The mountain climbers told us that the *vista* from the top of the
mountain was beautiful.

Word Study

Dictionary Use

Discuss the following questions.

1. When do you use a dictionary?

2. What kind of information does it give you?

3. When reading English, do you use a monolingual (English-English) or bilingual dictionary?

4. What are the advantages and disadvantages of a bilingual dictionary? Of a monolingual dictionary?

5. Are there times when you do not know what a word means and you do not use a dictionary?

The dictionary provides many kinds of information about words. Below is an excerpt from an English language dictionary. Study the entry carefully; notice how much information the dictionary presents under the word *discount*.

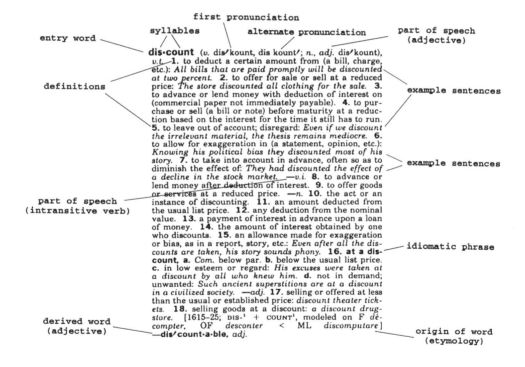

From *Random House Unabridged Dictionary* (New York: Random House, 1967), 563.

Your dictionary may use a different system of abbreviations or different pronunciation symbols. It is important for you to become familiar with your English dictionary and with the symbols it uses.

Look up *discount* in your dictionary and compare the entry to the entry above. Did you notice any differences? If so, what are they?

Exercise 1

Use the sample entry (page 69), the dictionary page (page 71),* and your own dictionary to answer the following questions. Your teacher may want you to work alone, in pairs, or in small groups.

1. When the dictionary gives more than one spelling or pronunciation, which one should you use?

   _____

2. Look at the sample entry.

   a. How many syllables are there in *discount?* _____

   b. What symbol does this dictionary use to separate the syllables? _____

   c. Why would you want to know where a word is divided into syllables? _____

   _____

3. *Discount* can be pronounced with the stress on either syllable when used as a verb.

   a. Which syllable is stressed in the first pronunciation of *discount?* _____

   b. Practice pronouncing *discount* with the stress on the first and on the second syllable.

4. How many different meanings are given for the verb *discount?* _____

   How many definitions are there for the noun *discount?* _____

5. T / F   *Discount* comes from Old German.

6. What are derived words? _____

   What is the derived adjective form of *discount?* _____

7. Where is the pronunciation guide on the dictionary page? _____

   a. What is the key word for the *ou* sound in *discount?* _____

   b. This key is the concise pronunciation key. Where do you think you might find the complete pronunciation key?

   _____

_____

*From *Random House Unabridged Dictionary, Second Edition* (New York: Random House, 1993), 478; Concise Pronunciation Key is from page 479.

atia, differing from Serbian chiefly in its use of the Latin alphabet. [1545–55; CROATI(A) + -AN]

croc (krok), *n. Informal.* crocodile. [1880–85; by shortening]

Cro•ce (krô′che), *n.* **Be•ne•det•to** (be′ne det′tô), 1866–1952, Italian statesman, philosopher, and historian.

cro•ce•in (krō′sē in), *n. Chem.* any of several acid azo dyes producing orange or scarlet colors. Also, **cro•ce•ine** (krō′sē in, -ēn′). [< L *croce(us)* saffron-colored (see CROCUS, -EOUS) + -IN[2]]

cro•chet (krō shā′; *Brit.* krō′shā, -shē), *n., v.,* **-cheted** (-shād′; *Brit.* -shād, -shēd), **-chet•ing** (-shā′ing; *Brit.* -shā ing, -shē ing). —*n.* **1.** needlework done with a needle having a small hook at one end for drawing the thread or yarn through intertwined loops. —*v.t., v.i.* **2.** to form by crochet. [1840–50; < F: knitting needle, lit., small hook, dim. of *croche, croc* < ME or Scand. See CROOK[1], -ET] —**cro•chet•er** (krō shā′ər; *Brit.* krō′shā-ər, -shē-), *n.*

crochet′ hook′, a needle with a hook at one end, used in crochet. Also called **crochet′ nee′dle.** [1840–50]

cro•chet•work (krō shā′wûrk′; *Brit.* krō′shā wûrk′, -shē-), *n.* needlework done by crocheting. [1855–60; CROCHET + WORK]

cro•cid•o•lite (krō sid′l īt′), *n. Mineral.* a bluish, asbestine variety of riebeckite. Also called **blue asbestos.** [1825–35; < Gk *krokid-* (s. of *krokís*) nap, wool + -O- + -LITE]

crock[1] (krok), *n.* **1.** an earthenware pot, jar, or other container. **2.** a fragment of earthenware; potsherd. [bef. 1000; ME *crokke,* OE *croc(c), crocca* pot; c. ON *krukka* jug]

crock[2] (krok), *n.* **1.** a person or thing that is old, decrepit, or broken-down. **2.** *Slang.* a person who complains about or insists on being treated for an imagined illness. **3.** an old ewe. **4.** an old worn-out horse. —*v.t.* **5.** *Brit. Slang.* to disable or injure. [1300–50; ME *crok* old ewe, perh. akin to CRACK (v.) and obs. *crack* whore; cf. LG *krakke* broken-down horse]

crock[3] (krok), *n.* **1.** *Brit. Dial.* soot; smut. **2.** excess surface dye from imperfectly dyed cloth. —*v.t.* **3.** *Brit. Dial.* to soil with soot. —*v.i.* **4.** (of cloth) to give off excess surface dye when rubbed. [1650–60; orig. uncert.]

crock[4] (krok), *n. Slang.* a lie; exaggeration; nonsense: *The entire story is just a crock.* [orig. unclear, though often taken as a euphemism for *a crock of shit*]

crocked (krokt), *adj. Slang.* drunk. [1925–30, *Amer.*; CROCK[2] + -ED[2]]

crock•er•y (krok′ə rē), *n.* crocks collectively; earthenware. [1710–20; CROCK[1] + -ERY]

crock•et (krok′it), *n. Archit.* a medieval ornament, usually in the form of a leaf that curves up and away from the supporting surface and returns partially upon itself. [1300–50; ME *croket* hook < AF, equiv. to *croc* hook (< Gmc; see CROOK[1]) + *-et* -ET. See CROCHET, CROTCHET]

crockets on coping of a gable

Crock•ett (krok′it), *n.* **David** (*Davy*), 1786–1836, U.S. frontiersman, politician, and folklore hero.

Crock•pot (krok′pot′), *Trademark.* a brand of electric slow cooker.

croc•o•dile (krok′ə dīl′), *n.* **1.** any of several crocodilians of the genus *Crocodylus,* found in sluggish waters and swamps of the tropics. **2.** any reptile of the order Crocodylia; crocodilian. **3.** the tanned skin or hide of these animals, used in the manufacture of luggage and accessories, as belts, shoes, and wallets. **4.** *Chiefly Brit.* a file of people, esp. schoolchildren, out for a walk. **5.** *Archaic.* a person who makes a hypocritical show of sorrow. [1250–1300; < L *crocodilus* < Gk *krokódeilos* crocodile, orig. a kind of lizard, said to be equiv. to *krók(ē)* pebble + *-o-* -O- + *drîlos, dreîlos* worm (though attested only in sense "penis"), with *r* lost by dissimilation *r.* ME *cocodrille* < ML *cocodrilus*] —**croc•o•dil•oid** (krok′ə-dil′oid, krok′ə di′loid), *adj.*

Nile crocodile, *Crocodylus niloticus,* length 20 ft. (6 m)

croc′odile bird′, an African courser, *Pluvianus aegyptius,* that often sits upon basking crocodiles and feeds on their insect parasites. [1865–70]

Croc′odile Riv′er, Limpopo.

croc′odile tears′, **1.** a hypocritical show of sorrow; insincere tears. **2.** *Pathol.* spontaneous tearing initiated by tasting or chewing food, occurring as a result of facial paralysis. [1555–65; so called from the the ancient belief that crocodiles shed tears while eating their victims]

croc•o•dil•i•an (krok′ə dil′ē ən), *n.* **1.** any reptile of the order Crocodylia, comprising the true crocodiles and the alligators, caimans, and gavials. —*adj.* **2.** of, like, or pertaining to a crocodile. **3.** hypocritical; insincere. [1625–35; CROCODILE + -IAN]

cro•co•ite (krō′kō īt′, krok′ō-), *n.* a yellow, orange, or red mineral, lead chromate, $PbCrO_4$, formed by replacement. Also called **cro•co•i•site** (krō′kō ə zīt′, krok′ō-). [1835–45; < Gk *krokó(eis)* saffron-colored + -ITE[1]; see CROCUS]

cro•cus (krō′kəs), *n., pl.* **-cus•es.** **1.** any of the small, bulbous plants of the genus *Crocus,* of the iris family, cultivated for their showy, solitary flowers, which are among the first to bloom in the spring. **2.** the flower or bulb of the crocus. **3.** a deep yellow; orangish yellow; saffron. **4.** Also called **cro′cus mar′tis** (mär′tis). a polishing powder consisting of iron oxide. [1350–1400; ME < L < Gk *krókos* saffron, crocus < Sem; cf. Ar *kurkum* saffron] —**cro′cused,** *adj.*

cro′cus sack′, *Southern U.S.* (*chiefly South Atlantic States*). a burlap bag. Also called **cro′cus bag′, croker sack.** [1780–90; orig. uncert.]
—**Regional Variation.** See **gunnysack.**

Croe•sus (krē′səs), *n., pl.* **-sus•es, -si** (-sī) for 2. **1.** died 546 B.C., king of Lydia 560–546: noted for his great wealth. **2.** a very rich man.

croft[1] (krôft, kroft), *n. Brit.* **1.** a small farm, esp. one worked by a tenant. **2.** a small plot of ground adjacent to a house and used as a kitchen garden, to pasture one or two cows, etc.; a garden large enough to feed a family or have commercial value. [bef. 1000; ME, OE: small field]

croft[2] (krôft, kroft), *n.* a small, portable filing cabinet of table height, having drop leaves for use as a table. [named after the Rev. Sir Herbert *Croft* (1757–1816), lexicologist, its inventor]

croft•er (krôf′tər, krof′-), *n. Brit.* a person who rents and works a small farm, esp. in Scotland or northern England. [1250–1300; ME; see CROFT[1], -ER[1]]

Crohn's′ disease′ (krōnz), *Pathol.* a chronic inflammatory bowel disease that causes scarring and thickening of the intestinal walls and frequently leads to obstruction. Also called **regional ileitis, regional enteritis.** [named after Burrill Bernard *Crohn* (1884–1983), U.S. physician, one of the authors of a description of the disease published in 1932]

croi•sette (krô set′, kro-), *n.* crossette.

crois•sant (*Fr.* krwä sän′; *Eng.* krə sänt′), *n., pl.* **-sants** (*Fr.* -sän′; *Eng.* -sänts′). a rich, buttery, crescent-shaped roll of leavened dough or puff paste. [1895–1900; < F: lit., CRESCENT]

Croix de Guerre (krwäd⁰ ger′), a French military award for heroism in battle. [1910–15; < F: lit., cross of war]

cro′ker sack′ (krō′kər). *Southern U.S.* (*chiefly Gulf States*). a crocus sack. Also called **cro′ker bag′.** [1875–80; *croker,* alter. of CROCUS]
—**Regional Variation.** See **gunnysack.**

Cro-Mag•non (krō mag′nən, -non, -man′yən), *n.* **1.** an Upper Paleolithic population of humans, regarded as the prototype of modern *Homo sapiens* in Europe. Skeletal remains found in an Aurignacian cave in southern France indicate that the Cro-Magnon had long heads, broad faces, and sunken eyes, and reached a height of approximately 5 ft. 9 in. (175 cm). See illus. under **hominid.** **2.** a member of the Cro-Magnon population. [1865–70; named after the cave (near Périgueux, France) where the first remains were found]

Cro•mer (krō′mər), *n.* **1st Earl of.** See **Baring, Evelyn.**

crom•lech (krom′lek), *n. Archaeol.* (no longer in technical use) a megalithic chamber tomb. Cf. **chamber tomb, dolmen, passage grave.** [1595–1605; < Welsh, equiv. to *crom* bent, curved, crooked (fem. of *crwm*) + *lech,* comb. form of *llech* flat stone]

cro′mo•lyn so′dium (krō′mə lin), *Pharm.* a substance, $C_{23}H_{14}Na_2O_{11}$, used as a preventive inhalant for bronchial asthma and hay fever. [1970–75; contr. and rearrangement of the chemical name]

cro•morne (krō môrn′, krə-), *n.* crumhorn. [1685–95; < F, alter. of G *Krumhorn;* see CRUMHORN]

Cromp•ton (kromp′tən), *n.* **Samuel,** 1753–1827, English inventor of the spinning mule.

Crom•well (krom′wəl, -wel; *for 1–3 also* krum′-), *n.* **1. Oliver,** 1599–1658, English general, Puritan statesman, and Lord Protector of England, Scotland, and Ireland 1653–58. **2.** his son, **Richard,** 1626–1712, English soldier, politician, Lord Protector of England 1658–59. **3. Thomas, Earl of Essex,** 1485?–1540, English statesman. **4.** a town in central Connecticut. 10,265.

Crom′well Cur′rent. See **Equatorial Countercurrent.** [after Townsend *Cromwell* (1922–58), U.S. oceanographer]

Crom•wel•li•an (krom wel′ē ən, krum-), *adj.* **1.** of, pertaining to, or characteristic of the politics, practices, etc., of Oliver Cromwell or of the Commonwealth and Protectorate. **2.** noting or pertaining to a style of English furnishings of the middle 17th century, characterized by austerity, the use of oak and leather, and simple, decorative moldings. [1715–25; CROMWELL + -IAN]

Cromwel′lian chair′, *Eng. Furniture.* an upright oaken chair, often with arms, having all pieces turned and a seat and back panel of leather or cloth attached with brass-headed nails. [1900–05]

crone (krōn), *n.* a withered, witchlike old woman. [1350–1400; ME < MD *croonie* old ewe < ONF *caronie* CARRION] —**cron′ish,** *adj.*

Cro•nin (krō′nin), *n.* **A(rchibald) J(oseph),** 1896–1981, Scottish novelist and physician in the U.S.

Cron•jé (*Du.* krôn′yā), *n.* **Piet Ar•nol•dus** (*Du.* pēt är-nôl′do͝os), 1835?–1911, Boer general.

cronk (krongk, krôngk), *adj. Australian Slang.* sick or feeble. [1875–80; < Yiddish or G *krank,* MHG *kranc* weak]

Cro•nus (krō′nəs), *n. Class. Myth.* a Titan, son of Uranus and Gaea, who was dethroned by his son Zeus. Cf. **Saturn.**

cro•ny (krō′nē), *n., pl.* **-nies.** a close friend or companion; chum. [1655–65; alleged to be university slang; perh. < Gk *chrónios* for a long time, long-continued, deriv. of *chrónos* time; cf. CHRONO-]
—**Syn.** pal, buddy.

cro•ny•ism (krō′nē iz′əm), *n.* the practice of favoring one's close friends, esp. in political appointments. [1830–40; CRONY + -ISM]

Cro•nyn (krō′nin), *n.* **Hume,** born 1911, Canadian actor in the U.S.

crook[1] (kro͝ok), *n.* **1.** a bent or curved implement, piece, appendage, etc.; hook. **2.** the hooked part of anything. **3.** an instrument or implement having a bent or curved part, as a shepherd's staff hooked at one end or the crosier of a bishop or abbot. **4.** a dishonest person, esp. a sharper, swindler, or thief. **5.** a bend, turn, or curve: *a crook in the road.* **6.** the act of crooking or bending. **7.** a pothook. **8.** Also called **shank.** a device on some musical wind instruments for changing the pitch, consisting of a piece of tubing inserted into the main tube. —*v.t.* **9.** to bend; curve; make a crook in. **10.** *Slang.* to steal, cheat, or swindle: *She crooked a ring from that shop.* —*v.i.* **11.** to bend; curve. [1125–75; ME *crok(e)* < ON *krāka* hook]

crook[2] (kro͝ok), *adj. Australian.* **1.** sick or feeble. **2.** ill-humored; angry. **3.** out of order; functioning improperly. **4.** unsatisfactory; disappointing. [1875–80; perh. alter. of CRONK]

crook•back (kro͝ok′bak′), *n.* a hunchback. [1400–50; late ME. See CROOK[1], BACK[1]] —**crook′backed′,** *adj.*

crook•ed (kro͝ok′id *for 1-4, 6;* kro͝okt *for 5*), *adj.* **1.** not straight; bending; curved: *a crooked path.* **2.** askew; awry: *The picture on the wall seems to be crooked.* **3.** deformed: *a man with a crooked back.* **4.** not straightforward; dishonest. **5.** bent and often raised or moved to one side, as a finger or neck. **6.** (of a coin) polygonal: *a crooked sixpence.* [1200–50; ME *croked;* see CROOK[1], -ED[2]] —**crook′ed•ly,** *adv.* —**crook′ed•ness,** *n.*
—**Syn. 1.** winding, devious, sinuous, flexuous, tortuous, spiral, twisted. **3.** misshapen. **4.** unscrupulous, knavish, tricky, fraudulent.

Crookes (kro͝oks), *n.* **Sir William,** 1832–1919, English chemist and physicist: discovered the element thallium and the cathode ray.

Crookes′ dark′ space′, *Physics.* the dark space between the cathode glow and the negative glow in a vacuum tube, occurring when the pressure is low. Also called **Crookes′ space′.** [1890–95; after Sir W. CROOKES]

crookes•ite (kro͝ok′sīt), *n.* a rare mineral, selenide of copper, thallium, and silver, $(Cu, Tl, Ag)_2Se$, occurring in steel-gray, compact masses. [1865–70; after Sir W. CROOKES; see -ITE[1]]

Crookes′ radiom′eter, *Optics.* radiometer (def. 1). [1880–85; after Sir W. CROOKES]

Crookes′ tube′, *Electronics.* a form of cathode-ray tube. [1880–85; after Sir W. CROOKES]

crook•neck (kro͝ok′nek′), *n.* **1.** any of several varieties of squash having a long, recurved neck. **2.** any plant bearing such fruit. [1750–60, *Amer.*; CROOK[1] + NECK]

crook′ raft′er. See **knee rafter.**

croon (kro͞on), *v.i.* **1.** to sing or hum in a soft, soothing voice: *to croon to a baby.* **2.** to sing in an evenly modulated, slightly exaggerated manner: *Popular singers began crooning in the 1930's.* **3.** to utter a low murmuring sound. **4.** *Scot. and North Eng.* **a.** to bellow; low. **b.** to lament; mourn. —*v.t.* **5.** to sing (a song) in a crooning manner. **6.** to lull by singing or humming to in a soft, soothing voice: *to croon a child to sleep.* —*n.* **7.** the act or sound of crooning. [1350–1400; ME *cronen* < MD: to lament] —**croon′er,** *n.* —**croon′ing•ly,** *adv.*

crop (krop), *n., v.,* **cropped** or (*Archaic*) **cropt; cropping.** —*n.* **1.** the cultivated produce of the ground, while growing or when gathered: *the wheat crop.* **2.** the yield of such produce for a particular season. **3.** the yield of some other product in a season: *the crop of diamonds.* **4.** a supply produced. **5.** a collection or group of persons or things appearing or occurring together: *this year's crop of students.* **6.** the stock or handle of a whip. **7.** Also called **riding crop.** a short riding whip consisting of a stock without a lash. **8.** Also called **craw.** *Zool.* **a.** a pouch in the esophagus of many birds, in which food is held for later digestion or for regurgitation to nestlings. **b.** a chamber or pouch in the foregut of arthropods and annelids for holding and partly crushing food. **9.** the act of cropping. **10.** a mark produced by clipping the ears, as of cattle. **11.** a close-cropped hair style. **12.** a head of hair so cut. **13.** an entire tanned hide of an animal. **14.** *Mining.* an outcrop of a vein or seam. —*v.t.* **15.** to cut off or remove the head or top of (a plant, grass, etc.). **16.** to cut off the ends or a part of: *to crop the ears of a dog.* **17.** to cut short. **18.** to clip the ears, hair, etc., of. **19.** *Photog.* to cut off or mask the unwanted parts of (a print or negative). **20.** to cause to bear a crop or crops. **21.** to graze off (the tops of plants, grass, etc.): *The sheep cropped the lawn.* —*v.i.* **22.** to bear or yield a crop or crops. **23.** to feed by cropping or

CONCISE PRONUNCIATION KEY: *act, cāpe, dâre, pärt; set, ēqual; if, īce; ox, ōver, ôrder, oil, bo͝ok, bo͞ot, out; up, ûrge; child; sing; shoe; thin, that;* zh as in *treasure.* ə = *a* as in *alone, e* as in *system, i* as in *easily, o* as in *gallop, u* as in *circus;* ⁰ as in *fire* (fī⁰r), *hour* (ou⁰r). l and n can serve as syllabic consonants, as in *cradle* (krād′l), and *button* (but′n). See the full key inside the front cover.

8. Now look for the pronunciation guide in your dictionary. Where is it located? _____

   Is it as easy to use as this one? _____

9. Dictionaries sometimes contain usage labels such as "regional," "informal," and "slang." Why are these labels useful?

   _____

10. Read the definitions of *discount.* Below are several sentences in which *discount* is used. In the space provided, write the number of the definition for that usage.

    ___ a. Because it is the end of the ski season, you can buy most ski equipment at a *discount.*

    ___ b. Most stores know that if they do not *discount* all of the ski equipment, they will not be able to sell it.

    ___ c. Because he never told me the truth before, I *discounted* his story about the accident.

Exercise 2

In this exercise you will scan the dictionary page (p. 71) to find the answers to specific questions. These questions will introduce you to several kinds of information to be found in a dictionary. Read each question, find the answer as quickly as possible, then write it in the space provided. Your teacher may want you to work individually and then discuss your answers with classmates in pairs or small groups.

1. The two words at the top of the page are called guide words. They are the first and last words defined on the page; only words that occur alphabetically between *croc* and *crop* will be found on this page.

   a. T / F   You will find *crook* on this page.

   b. T / F   You will find *critical* on this page.

   c. T / F   You will find *cropper* on this page.

2. How many syllables are there in *crocidolite?* _____ What are they? _____

3. Which syllable is stressed in *cronyism?* _____

4. Look at the entry for *crocus.*

   a. T / F   A *crocus* is a type of small crocodile.

   b. What is the key word that tells you how to pronounce the *o* in *crocus?* _____

   c. What is the key word that tells you how to pronounce the *u* in *crocus?* _____

   d. Pronounce *crocus* aloud.

5. How do the British pronounce *crochet?* _____

6. Write the correct form of the italicized words in the sentences below.

   a. Yesterday I _____ the twin's hair. Tomorrow I'll *crop* yours.

   b. "Those pictures look *crooked* to me." "You're right, they are hung _____ ."

   c. The mayor has been criticized for his *cronyism*. It seems that no matter what the job is, he always finds one of his friends to take it. This office, for example, is full of his _____ .

7. T / F   Samuel Crompton is an American inventor who lives in Boston.

8. Write the languages from which the following words came:

   a. *croissant* _____

   b. *cronk* _____

   c. *crochet* _____

   d. *crony* _____

9. What word must you look up to find the meaning of *riding crop?* _____

10. a. How many synonyms are listed for *crooked?* _____

    b. How many antonyms? _____

Sentence Study

Comprehension

Read the following sentences carefully.* The questions that follow are designed to test your comprehension of complex grammatical structures. Select the best answer.

1. Despite all the money it spent on advertising the new car, the company isn't having much success selling it.
   What do we know about the company?
   ___ a. It spent a lot of money on advertising.
   ___ b. Its advertisements have had much success.
   ___ c. It has had a lot of success selling its new car.
   ___ d. It has had a lot of success selling its advertising.

2. So many of the test questions are so difficult that no student should feel ashamed of not knowing the answers.
   What does the writer say about students?
   ___ a. They should feel ashamed if they can't answer the difficult test questions.
   ___ b. They should know the answers to many of the difficult questions on this test.
   ___ c. No students will do well on the test.
   ___ d. They should not feel ashamed if they miss some questions on this test.

3. The project would have failed even with Theresa's help.
   What do we know about the project?
   ___ a. It failed because Theresa didn't help.
   ___ b. Theresa did not help, and it failed.
   ___ c. Theresa helped, so it didn't fail.
   ___ d. It will fail without Theresa's help.

4. It is surprising that doctors don't know whether many drugs found effective for men will also help women.
   What does the writer think is surprising?
   ___ a. That many drugs that help men also help women
   ___ b. That many drugs that help men don't help women
   ___ c. That doctors don't know whether some drugs help men
   ___ d. That doctors don't know how some drugs affect women

5. As a doctor at Harper Hospital, Susan Wilson is a part of a team of cancer experts advising other doctors about their patients and teaching medical students.
   Who is Susan Wilson?
   ___ a. A doctor who is an expert on cancer
   ___ b. A cancer patient whose doctor is at Harper Hospital
   ___ c. A medical student working with cancer experts
   ___ d. An adviser who works part time at Harper Hospital

---

*For an introduction to sentence study, see Unit 1.

6. If it goes the way the boss hopes it will, John will start his new job no later than June 1, when Ellen leaves.
   The boss wants . . .
   ___ a. Ellen to leave after June 1.
   ___ b. John to start by June 1.
   ___ c. to go away before June 1.
   ___ d. to start his new job by June 1.

7. Aside from her work with the movie director D. W. Griffith, Lillian Gish's acting in *The Wind* is her best.
   Gish's best performance was . . .
   ___ a. in *The Wind.*
   ___ b. aside from her work.
   ___ c. with D. W. Griffith.
   ___ d. not as good as D. W. Griffith's.

8. Sam, the worst player on the team, passed the ball to Pete who, as the best player, had a better chance to score.
   What happened in the game?
   ___ a. Sam got a better chance to score.
   ___ b. Pete threw the ball to the best player.
   ___ c. Sam threw the ball to the best player.
   ___ d. Pete threw the ball to the worst player.

9. For J. D. Woods, the long-term worry is not that there will be too many airplanes at the small airport, but too few.
   J. D. Woods worries that . . .
   ___ a. there will not be enough airplanes.
   ___ b. there will be too many airplanes.
   ___ c. the airport will be too small.
   ___ d. it will take a long time to land at the airport.

10. With the exception of AT&T, each of the many long-distance telephone companies in this country is a relative youngster.
    What does the author say about AT&T?
    ___ a. It is a relatively young company.
    ___ b. It is older than the other long-distance companies.
    ___ c. It no longer operates in this country.
    ___ d. It has a long relationship with other companies.

11. The thing that surprised me is not the number of attacks by lions on humans in the Vancouver area but how really few there have been.
    What does the author say about the attacks?
    ___ a. He expected there would be more.
    ___ b. He expected there would be fewer.
    ___ c. He didn't expect there would be any.
    ___ d. He isn't sure how many there were.

12. Although the dance looks easy to do, it isn't; just ask John!
    What do we know about the dance?
    ___ a. It isn't easy to do.
    ___ b. It is easy to do.
    ___ c. John knows how to do it.
    ___ d. John asked how to do it.

Paragraph Reading

Restatement and Inference

The paragraphs in this exercise are taken from the book *Helen Keller: Crusader for the Blind and Deaf.* So that you will know something about Helen before you begin reading, here is a summary of the book that appears on its cover:

> Helen Keller was born in 1880. From the age of a year and a half, she could not hear. She could not see, and she did not speak. She lived in a dark and lonely world—until Annie Sullivan came to teach her. Annie spelled letters and words in Helen's hand and made Helen realize she could "talk" to people. Helen threw herself into her studies. She decided to teach others about the special training deaf and blind children need. Helen traveled all over the world and raised money to start schools for deaf and blind children. Her courage and desire to help others overcome their problems earned her the respect and love of people all over the world.

Before You Begin   1. Have you heard of Helen Keller before?
2. What do you know about her based on your previous knowledge and information from the summary paragraph you just read?

Each paragraph below about Helen Keller's life is followed by four statements. The statements are of four types:

1. Some of the statements are restatements of ideas in the original paragraph. They give the same information in a different way.

2. Some of the statements are inferences (conclusions) that can be drawn from the information given in the paragraph.

3. Some of the statements are not true based on the information given.

4. Some of the statements cannot be proved true or false based on the information given.

Put a check (✓) next to all restatements and inferences (types 1 and 2). Note: do not check a statement that is true of itself but cannot be inferred from the paragraph. There is not always a single correct set of answers. Be prepared to discuss your choices with your classmates.

Example

One morning Helen woke early. She could not see the daylight, but she smelled bacon and eggs cooking. She knew it was time to get up. Her mother hurried Helen through breakfast and dressed her carefully. Helen did not know what was happening. Still she felt excited. When her father lifted her into the carriage she wondered where they were going.

___ a. Helen could not see, but there was nothing wrong with her sense of smell.
___ b. Helen had bacon and eggs every day for breakfast.
___ c. There was something unusual about this morning.
___ d. Helen was not very smart.

Explanation

✓ a. This is a restatement of the second sentence. Helen could not see the daylight, but she could smell the bacon (there was nothing wrong with her sense of smell).

___ b. This cannot be inferred from the paragraph. Helen obviously recognizes bacon as something she eats for breakfast, but we do not know that she eats it every day.

✓ c. This can be inferred from the paragraph. Helen did not know what was happening. Also, the fact that Helen's mother wants her to finish breakfast quickly but dresses her carefully suggests that something important or special is about to happen. Helen feels excited, and she and her father are going someplace.

___ d. This is false. Although she is blind, Helen is able to use the other information around her (smells and feelings) to understand the world.

Paragraph 1

Whatever they did, Annie spelled letters into Helen's hand. When they petted the cat, Annie spelled "C-A-T." Helen quickly learned to copy the movements of Annie's fingers. "Helen is like a clever little monkey," Annie wrote. "She has learned the signs to ask for what she wants but she has no idea that she is spelling words."

___ a. Finger spelling is only for saying what you want.

___ b. Helen didn't know that the sign for cat spelled the word for cat.

___ c. Monkeys can copy actions without understanding their real meaning.

___ d. People who make signs don't understand what they are doing.

But Helen needed to learn more. One morning while cold water poured over Helen's hand, Annie spelled the word W-A-T-E-R in the other hand. Suddenly Helen understood that this was a word and pointed to things around her, wanting to know how they were all spelled.

Paragraph 2

Helen and Annie were both excited. They ran to the house to find Mrs. Keller. When Helen threw herself in her mother's arms, Annie spelled "M-O-T-H-E-R" into her hand. When Helen nodded to show that she understood there were tears of happiness in Mrs. Keller's eyes.

___ a. Helen understood that the finger spelling of M-O-T-H-E-R was the word for the person, mother.

___ b. Helen's mother was happy because Helen hugged her.

___ c. Helen's mother was a very emotional person.

___ d. Helen's mother understood that Helen would now be able to learn.

Paragraphs adapted from *Helen Keller: Crusader for the Blind and Deaf,* by Stewart and Polly Anne Graff (New York: Dell Young Yearling/Bantam Doubleday Dell, 1965), 7, 13–14, 17, 28, 30, 36, 39–40, 41, 46–48, 56–57.

Now Helen had discovered language. But there were other things that Helen needed to learn as well. Helen had become used to doing things her own way. For example, she ate with her fingers and she refused to do anything that was difficult or new.

Paragraph 3

At the dinner table, Annie made Helen sit in her own chair and eat from her own plate. Helen was furious. When Annie gave her a spoon, Helen threw it on the floor and kicked the table. They spent a whole afternoon fighting while Annie insisted that Helen fold her napkin before leaving the table.

___ a. Annie believed in always being neat and clean.
___ b. Annie did not love Helen.
___ c. Helen did not usually sit at the table and eat from her plate.
___ d. Folding the napkin represented something important to Annie.

Annie became Helen's special teacher and lifelong friend. When Helen was eight years old, it was time for Helen (and Annie) to go to school. Helen learned to read braille, the system of raised dots that blind people read with their fingers.

Paragraph 4

In Helen's second year at Perkins school she heard of a little blind-deaf boy named Tommy Stringer. He had no family and no one to teach him.

___ a. Helen spent only two years at the Perkins school.
___ b. Tommy Stringer probably did not know how to read braille.
___ c. Helen could hear Tommy Stringer speak.
___ d. Tommy Stringer was at Perkins school when Helen heard of him.

Helen helped raise money for Tommy Stringer to come to Perkins school. All the while, Helen continued to study. When she was ten years old, she was taught to speak by Sarah Fuller, a teacher at the Horace Mann School for the Deaf in Boston.

Paragraph 5

First Helen would put her hand on Miss Fuller's face when she talked. Then Helen would try to copy the way Miss Fuller's lips and tongue moved. It was hard work. Over and over Helen tried to make sounds, but she could not hear the sounds she made. She did not know when her voice sounded strange to others. After each lesson, Helen practiced with Annie. At last, one day, she could speak a whole sentence that Annie could understand.

___ a. Helen could not feel Miss Fuller's face very well.
___ b. Helen's voice sometimes sounded strange to others.
___ c. Annie could always understand what Helen was trying to say.
___ d. It was hard work learning to talk.

When she was in her teens, Helen decided that she wanted to attend college. To prepare, she studied hard at school and had private teachers. She learned to use a braille typewriter to keep her study notes and a regular typewriter too for school papers. Helen entered Radcliffe College in 1900. Her special teacher, Annie Sullivan, went with her.

Paragraph 6   When college classes began, Annie sat next to Helen. She spelled what the teachers said into Helen's hand. Annie looked up words in the dictionary for Helen. She read Helen books that were not printed in braille.

___ a. Annie read books aloud to Helen.
___ b. Annie finger spelled dictionary definitions for Helen.
___ c. Annie finger spelled some books for Helen.
___ d. Annie did Helen's homework for her.

After graduating from college, Helen had to decide whether to become a teacher herself or to work for blind and deaf children in other ways.

Paragraph 7   Helen wanted to pass on the gift of teaching that Annie had given her. But at last she decided she could help best by writing and lecturing. "I can tell more people about the special training that deaf and blind children need," she told Annie. "I can teach them what you taught me—that children must not be treated differently because they are blind and deaf. They can learn to work and be happy."

___ a. Helen could teach by writing and lecturing.
___ b. Deaf and blind children are not different from other children.
___ c. Helen could not speak in public because her voice was too strange.
___ d. Helen gave special training to blind and deaf children.

Helen worked to try to get more books printed in braille because she knew that many blind people did not have enough to read. She went to Washington, D.C. to ask the U.S. government for help.

Paragraph 8   In 1913 there was important news. The National Library for the Blind was started. Helen and Annie went to Washington for the opening. President Taft of the United States was present at the opening of the new library.

___ a. President Taft began the library.
___ b. The library was in Washington, D.C.
___ c. The library had braille books.
___ d. The library mostly had books about blind people.

During one period, when Helen and Annie needed money, Helen acted in a movie about her life, and she and Annie appeared in theaters. Finally, they earned the money they needed.

Paragraph 9   Now Helen could work again for others. She was happy with news from Washington. Congress had voted money for many more books for the blind. Some could be played on records. They were called "talking books."

___ a. Talking books were a way for the deaf and blind to hear.
___ b. The library for the blind was only for blind people who could hear.
___ c. The library for the blind had only a few books before.
___ d. The library for the blind was supported by the U.S. government.

But Helen wanted to help people all over the world. She had already helped children in Japan, and the Emperor himself had thanked her. Now she hoped to help more children worldwide.

Paragraph 10   In May 1959, the Helen Keller World Crusade was begun at the United Nations building in New York City. It would help blind and deaf children all over the world. Helen was very proud. She had lived through two terrible world wars. She had always hoped for world peace. Now it made her happy to know that people of different countries and races would work together to help children.

___ a. Helen Keller did not believe in war.
___ b. The Helen Keller World Crusade helped all blind and deaf children who needed help.
___ c. Before the Helen Keller World Crusade, some blind and deaf children had no help.
___ d. Before the Helen Keller World Crusade, people throughout the world had not worked together to help children.

Discourse Focus

Careful Reading / Drawing Inferences

Readers all around the world love mystery stories. Have you heard of Sherlock Holmes? Have you read some of the cases of Agatha Christie's famous detectives Miss Marple and Hercule Poirot? Do you have a favorite character in mysteries written in your native language?

One reason mysteries are so popular is that reading a mystery story is a kind of game with questions. Readers try to find out why something happened or who did something. In one type of mystery story, a famous detective is called to try to answer questions that no one else has been able to answer. Readers watch the detective study the problem. They learn all that the detective learns. The game for readers is to understand what happened based only on the information given.

The stories that follow are mysteries solved by a police detective named Dr. Haledjian. He is known for solving the most difficult cases. As you read each story, see if you are as good a detective as Dr. Haledjian. Read each mystery carefully, and then answer the question that follows it. Your teacher may want you to work with your classmates to answer the question. Be prepared to defend your answers with details from the story. (If you have trouble solving a mystery, you'll find additional clues on pages 85–86.)

Mystery 1: The Case of the Big Deal

Dr. Haledjian had just ordered a drink at the bar in the Las Vegas hotel when a young stranger with sun-bleached golden hair and suntanned cheeks sat down next to him.

After asking for a drink, the sunburned young man looked towards Dr. Haledjian. "I'm Clive Vance," he said pleasantly. "It's sure great to be back in civilization."

The famous detective introduced himself. "You've been out in the desert for a long time, have you?"

"Got back yesterday," said Vance. "Washed the dust out of my ears, and had a barber shave off seven months of beard and cut my hair. Then I bought all new clothes. I didn't even have to pay for them yet. All I had to do was to show the owner of the clothes store this piece of paper," he said as he showed Haledjian a report that showed he had found gold. "I sure am ready to celebrate."

"You found gold in the desert?"

"Right you are." Vance rubbed his suntanned chin thoughtfully. He lowered his voice to a whisper:

"Listen," he said. "If I can find someone to pay to get the gold out of the ground, I'll make enough to buy ten hotels like this one.

"Of course," he added, "I'm not trying to interest *you* Doctor. But if you know somebody who'd like to make a million dollars or two, let me know. I'm staying in room 210. I can't talk about all the details here, you understand."

Mysteries are adapted from *Two-Minute Mysteries,* by Donald J. Sobol (New York: Scholastic Book Services, 1967): "The Big Deal," 13–14; "The Case of the Blackmailer," 17–18; "The Case of the Bogus Robbery," 19–20; "The Case of the Buried Treasure," 27–28; "The Case of the Dentist's Patient," 49–50.

"I understand," said Haledjian, "that you should tell a better story if you want some fool to give you money."

How did Dr. Haledjian know that Vance was lying?

Mystery 2: The Case of the Lying Gardener

"Dr. Haledjian, I have had some problems since my father died and left me all his money," said Thomas Hunt. "Do you remember Martin, the man who took care of my father's gardens for many years?"

"A smiling, overly polite fellow, right?" said Haledjian as he poured his young friend a drink.

"That's the man. I told him his job ended the day my father died. Well, three days ago he came to my office, smiling as always, and demanded that I pay him $100,000.

"He claimed to have been taking care of the trees outside my father's room when Dad prepared another will, leaving all of his money to his brother in New Zealand."

"You believed him?"

"I admit the news surprised me. Sometime during the last week in November, Dad and I had argued about my plans to marry Elizabeth. Dad did not want us to marry, so it seemed possible that he had decided to change his will and leave all his money to his brother instead of to me.

"Martin said he had my father's second will and offered to sell it to me and keep it a secret for one hundred thousand dollars. He told me that the second will would be considered legal because it was dated November 31, the day after the will that left my father's money to me.

"I refused to be blackmailed. He tried to bargain, asking $50,000, and then $25,000."

"You paid nothing, I hope?" asked Haledjian.

"Nothing at all. I told him to get out of my house."

"Quite right," approved Haledjian. "The story is clearly not true!"

What was Martin's mistake?

Mystery 3: The Case of the Fake Robbery

Mrs. Sidney was so rich that she could do almost anything she wanted, but she could not do what she wanted most. Although she had tried many times, she never had been able to fool the great detective, Dr. Haledjian.

Haledjian knew she was trying once more when at two o'clock in the morning he got a call from Mrs. Sidney who cried, "My jewels have been stolen."

Entering Mrs. Sidney's bedroom, the famous detective closed the door and quickly looked around the room.

The window was open. Across the room, to the left of the bed, stood a table with a book and two lighted candles. The candles had burned down to three inches and had dripped down the side facing the windows.

A bell lay on the thick green carpet. The top drawer of the bedside table was open.

"What happened?" asked Haledjian.

"I was reading in bed by candlelight when the wind blew the window open," said Mrs. Sidney. "I could feel a cool breeze, so I rang the bell to call James, the butler, to come shut it.

"Before he arrived, a man with a gun entered and forced me to tell him where I kept my jewels. As he put them in his pocket, James entered. The thief tied both of us up with pairs of my stockings.

"As he left, I asked him to close the window because the wind was so cold. He just laughed and left it open.

"It took James 20 minutes to free himself and untie me. I will have a terrible cold in the morning!" said Mrs. Sidney.

"Congratulations," said Haledjian, "on a clever, well-planned crime; and you have been fair to give me the clue that proves the crime never happened."

How did Haledjian know that there had been no robbery?

Mystery 4: The Case of the Buried Treasure

"From the look on your face, I would guess you are about to get rich quick," said Dr. Haledjian.

"Clever of you to notice," said Bertie Tilford, a young man who was too lazy to work. "If I had just $10,000, I could make a million! Do you have $10,000 to invest?"

"What's your trick this time?" demanded Haledjian. "Gold coins at the bottom of the ocean? Treasure, gold and silver buried under the sands of some desert island?"

Bertie opened a bag and pulled out a shining silver candlestick. "Pure silver," he sang. "Look at what's written on the bottom."

Haledjian turned the candlestick over and read the name *Lady North.* "Wasn't that the ship that sank in 1956?"

"The *Lady North* sank, but not all the sailors on board died as most people believed," replied Bertie. "Four men escaped with a fortune in silver before the ship sank in the storm.

"They hid the silver in a cave in the side of a mountain on Gull Island," continued Bertie. "But the storm started a rock slide and closed off the entrance, burying three of the sailors inside the cave. The fourth, a man named Pembroot, escaped. Pembroot's been trying to raise $10,000 to buy the land on which the cave is located."

"You provide the money, the cave will be opened, and the treasure will be divided between you and Pembroot. Wonderful," said Haledjian. "Only how do you know Pembroot isn't trying to trick you?"

"Earlier tonight he took me to the cave," said Bertie. "This sack was half buried in the bushes, and I nearly broke my leg tripping over it. I took one look and brought the candlestick here immediately. You've got to agree it's real silver."

"It is," admitted Haledjian. "And there's no doubt that Pembroot placed it near the cave to fool you."

How did Haledjian know that the silver candlestick did not come from the Lady North?

Mystery 5: The Case of the Dentist's Patient

Dr. Chris Williams, a London-born New York dentist, was preparing to check the teeth of her patient, David Hoover. Silently the door behind her opened. A gloved hand holding a gun appeared.

Two shots sounded. Mr. Hoover fell over, dead.

"We've got a suspect," Inspector Winters told Dr. Haledjian at his office an hour later. "The elevator operator took a nervous man to the 15th floor—Dr. Williams has one of six offices on the floor—a few moments before the shooting. The description fits John Burton.

"Burton was recently let out of prison," continued the inspector. "I had a police officer go to his hotel and bring him in. Burton thinks I just want to ask him about whether he has been following the rules since he left prison."

Burton was brought into the room. "What's this all about?" he demanded angrily.

"Have you ever heard of Dr. Williams?" asked the inspector.

"No, why?"

"David Hoover was shot to death less than two hours ago as he sat in a chair in Dr. Williams' office."

"I was sleeping all afternoon."

"An elevator operator says he took a man who looks like you to the 15th floor just before the shots."

"It wasn't me," shouted Burton. "I look like a lot of guys. I haven't been near a dentist's office since I was in prison. This Williams, I bet she never saw me, so what can you prove?"

"Enough to send you to prison for the rest of your life," exclaimed Dr. Haledjian.

Why was Haledjian so sure that Burton was the murderer?

Additional Clues

If you had trouble solving any of the mysteries, here are additional clues. True/False items are indicated by a T / F before a statement.

Mystery 1: Try answering these questions:

   a. Why was Clive Vance's hair blond?

   b. T / F   Clive had just had his beard shaved off.

   c. T / F   Clive's face was brown from the sun.

Now can you explain why Dr. Haledjian did not believe Vance?

Mystery 2: No luck? Try these questions:

    a. What was the date of the will that Martin had?
    b. Why is the date important to the solution of the mystery?
    c. How many days are there in November?

Mystery 3: Do you want some more clues?

    a. How long had the windows been open?
    b. What did the candles look like when Haledjian came into the room? Where had the wax dripped?
    c. T / F   The wind was blowing into the room.

Mystery 4: Maybe answering these questions will help:

    a. Where had the candlestick been since 1956?
    b. What was the condition of the candlestick Bertie had?
    c. What happens to the appearance of silver as time passes?

Mystery 5: If you're not sure, answer these questions:

    a. Does Burton know whether Williams is a man or woman?
    b. How does Burton know that Williams is a dentist and not a foot doctor?

Reading Selection 1

Newspaper Article

Before You Begin   1. If you could live anywhere, where would it be?

2. What kind of a house would you live in?

These are questions that Ernest Dittemore had thought about before his house burned down. When that happened he knew what he wanted to do. . . . (Your teacher may want you to do the Vocabulary from Context exercise on pages 89–90 before you begin.)

The Seattle Times/Seattle Post-Intelligencer

Farmer Calls Hole His Home

KENDALL J. WILLS, ASSOCIATED PRESS

1   When fire destroyed Ernest Dittemore's six-room farmhouse 18 years ago, his neighbors got together to buy the 60-year-old bachelor a trailer house.

Dittemore was grateful. He thanked his friends, filled the trailer with food, then spent the night in a 4-by-10-foot hole that he'd dug in the ground with a shovel.

2   Now just months before his 78th birthday, Dittemore still goes into the hole every night, using the trailer just for storage.

"I'd been thinking about living underground for quite a while, even before the house burned," Dittemore said. "It's a lot easier to heat."

3   His underground house has dirt walls and a dirt floor. He sleeps on a bed of newspapers and uses a wood-burning stove for heat.

A skylight built into the piece of concrete that is his ceiling has been darkened by the smoke, but it still

Ernest Dittemore wipes some dirt from his eye while tending his 80-acre Kansas farm, where he lives in a hole in the ground that he dug with a shovel after his house burned down, 18 years ago.
Associated Press

allows a little light in. There are no lights or electricity.

4   Dittemore is unconcerned about anybody who thinks he's odd. "As long as I like it, that's all that matters. I don't ask them what they think, and

I don't care," he said.

At first people nearby in the small town of Troy, about 15 miles west of St. Joseph, Missouri, were confused. But they seem to have accepted Dittemore's unusual lifestyle.

From the *Seattle Times/Seattle Post-Intelligencer,* March 7, 1993, A8.

Some affectionately call him the "cave man of Doniphan County."

5 To get to his underground room, Dittemore lifts the ceiling. Steps lead to the floor 7 feet below. He says it's comfortable enough, even when the temperature outside goes below freezing.

6 Two bad knees force Dittemore to use canes made from tree branches to get around. Even so, he takes care of 30 head of cattle, six horses, a dozen chickens, and a few cats and dogs on his 80-acre farm.

7 His money from Social Security* and cattle sales is enough to pay for what he needs.

Neighbors say Dittemore is not crazy. He sends birthday and Christmas cards to his relatives and friends. And when his legs were better, he helped them on their farms.

Neighbor Larry Jones returns this favor by bringing Dittemore food for him and his animals.

8 Jim Gilmore, who grew up on the farm next to Dittemore's, said his friend is just different, not a hermit trying to hide from the real world.

"A lot of guys you read about, they seem to get mean living by themselves," Gilmore said. "But Ernie is the nicest guy you'll ever meet.

"One day we'll find him dead in the hole. But he'll die happy."

*Social Security: A U.S. government program that gives money monthly to older people and those who are not able to work.

Comprehension

Indicate if each statement below is true (T) or false (F) according to your understanding of the article.

1. T / F   Ernest Dittemore lives in a 6-room farmhouse.

2. T / F   Dittemore is 60 years old.

3. T / F   Sometimes Dittemore lives in a trailer given to him by his neighbors.

4. T / F   Dittemore's hole is 10 feet deep.

5. T / F   There is a wood-burning stove in Dittemore's hole.

6. T / F   There is a little electric light in Dittemore's hole.

7. T / F   Because of his bad knees, Dittemore is no longer able to take care of his farm.

8. T / F   Dittemore's neighbors think he is trying to hide from the world.

Critical Reading

Below is a list of words and phrases. You will decide which of these describe Ernest Dittemore. There is no single correct set of answers. Your teacher may want you to discuss this exercise in pairs or small groups. Be prepared to support your choices with examples from your personal experiences and the text.

1. First, check (✓) all the descriptions below that Ernest Dittemore's *neighbors* would use to describe him. Be sure you can support your choices with parts of the article you have read.

___ crazy   ___ nice   ___ a hermit
___ odd   ___ lonely   ___ a farmer
___ mean   ___ happy   ___ a good neighbor

2. Now look at the list again. Check (✓) all those descriptions that *you* think describe Ernest Dittemore. Again, be prepared to defend your choices.

— crazy   — nice   — a hermit
— odd   — lonely   — a farmer
— mean   — happy   — a good neighbor

3. Were your answers the same in question 1 and question 2? If not, why not?

4. Why do you think this article was written? That is, why would readers find this article interesting? Do you think Ernest Dittemore would find this article interesting?

Discussion/Composition

Choose one of the statements below and tell why you agree or disagree with it. Use information from the article and from your own experience.

a. We should all be more like Ernest Dittemore. He is doing what he wants to do. He lives the way he wants to live, and he doesn't hurt anyone.

b. Ernest Dittemore is crazy.

c. Sometimes we need to save people from themselves. Ernest Dittemore should not be allowed to live alone in his dangerous home.

Vocabulary from Context

The vocabulary in the exercise below is taken from "Farmer Calls Hole His Home." Use the context provided to decide on meanings for the italicized words. Write a definition, synonym, or description in the space provided.

1. _____ John never wanted to get married; he always said he enjoyed being a *bachelor.*

2. _____ Mary couldn't afford a regular house, so she lived in a *trailer.* It had everything a house has—bathroom, bedrooms, kitchen—but, of course, it had wheels.

3. _____ The ground was very hard and full of rocks. The workers broke three *shovels* trying to dig holes.

4. _____ Doug missed seeing the stars at night when he was indoors. At first, he tried painting a picture of the sky on his *ceiling,* so he could lie in bed at night and see the stars. But then he had a better idea. He made a

5. _____ hole through his ceiling and roof, and he put in a glass *skylight.* Now he had more light in the daytime and could watch the stars at night.

6. _____   Most sidewalks are made of *concrete*. When they are being built, children can write their names in the wet concrete so people can see them forever.

7. _____   Celia owns so many things that there isn't enough room in her house for all of them. Instead of keeping her car in the garage, she uses the garage for *storage*.

8. _____   Bill always worries about what other people think. In contrast, Sue is completely *unconcerned* about the opinions of others.

9. _____   Paula is a warm, loving person who likes all of her students. Every morning she greets each of them *affectionately.*

10. _____   Barb helped Mary by giving her a ride to work. The next day, Mary returned the *favor* and drove Barb.

11. _____   Ken lives by himself and tries never to see other human beings. Although he is a *hermit,* he isn't lonely.

12. _____   The children don't like Mr. Jones because he is so *mean.* In fact, because of his hateful ways, he has no friends.

Reading Selection 2

 Popular Social Science

Before You Begin   T / F People should never say things that aren't true.

1. Check (✓) all those situations below in which you would say something that is not true. When you are finished, compare your responses to your classmates'.

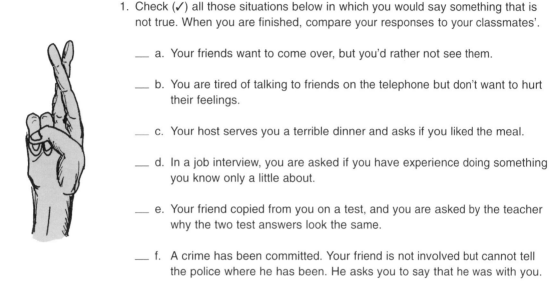

___ a. Your friends want to come over, but you'd rather not see them.

___ b. You are tired of talking to friends on the telephone but don't want to hurt their feelings.

___ c. Your host serves you a terrible dinner and asks if you liked the meal.

___ d. In a job interview, you are asked if you have experience doing something you know only a little about.

___ e. Your friend copied from you on a test, and you are asked by the teacher why the two test answers look the same.

___ f. A crime has been committed. Your friend is not involved but cannot tell the police where he has been. He asks you to say that he was with you.

___ g. You are separated from your husband or wife, and you think it will be a big problem if your friends or family find out.

2. A *lie* is an untrue statement. But people disagree whether all untrue statements are bad and whether all untrue statements should be called lies. Some people think that there is a difference between "little lies" and "lies." And some think that "little lies" shouldn't be thought of as lies at all. Look again at the items you checked in question 1. Put an *L* next to all those that you think are "little lies." Would you call these untrue statements "lies"?

Read the following article to find out why people "lie." Your teacher may want you to do the Vocabulary from Context exercise 1 on page 95 before you begin.

Lies Are So Commonplace, They Almost Seem Like the Truth

Terry Lee Goodrich
Fort Worth Star-Telegram

1   Everyone lies. Little lies, perhaps, which may not cause serious problems, but still they are lies. We fudge on how old we are, how much we weigh, what we are paid. Some people tell their children that Santa Claus will come on Christmas Eve.

2   Consider the last time you got a phone call from someone you didn't want to talk to. Did you perhaps claim falsely that you were just on your way out the door? That your newborn (you're childless) needed you?

   Did you ever promise anyone, "We'll do lunch," when you knew that you'd never get together?

   Did you ever reach for the phone to call in sick to work, then leap from bed to enjoy the day?

   Did you ever tell someone you owed money to that the check was in the mail when it wasn't?

3   Few behaviors serve as many purposes as lying. We grow up to use lies—or at least half truths—to avoid things that should be done, to get people to believe us, to get what we want, to buy time, to end conversations, to keep relationships going.

   "Lying is also exciting," said Margaret Summy, a professional counselor in Fort Worth, Texas. "It's living dangerously. Besides, we all want to be important, so we change our stories to make them more interesting."

4   "We also lie to make people agree with us, without really realizing that we're doing so," said clinical psychologist David Welsh.

   "In working with relationships such as parent-child or husband-wife, each person has a different memory, one which helps them. They'll accuse each other of lying," he said. "But both are telling their own understanding of the truth."

5   Perhaps the most understandable reason people lie is so they don't hurt others' feelings. Most guests at a dinner party wouldn't want to say that they didn't like a specially prepared meal, even if it was terrible.

6   But even though people lie for good reasons, lying can be harmful. If we act on false information, we can be hurt. If we lie and are discovered, it can destroy the trust necessary for strong relationships. Besides, lying is hard on the brain because one lie leads to another, and we always have to remember our false story. In his "Discourses on Government," Algernon Sidney said, "Liars ought to have good memories."

7   For most of us, though, lying is hard on us physically. We breathe faster, our hearts beat harder, and our blood pressure goes up.

   The truth can be hard on the body, too, of course—especially if we're admitting to a lie. Just about the most difficult thing for any human being to do is to tell others that he or she lied to them. It's very stressful.

Comprehension

Exercise 1

Check (✓) all those statements below with which the author would probably agree.

1. __ All untruths are lies.

2. __ Everyone lies.

3. __ We learn to lie as we are growing up.

Adapted from "Lies Are So Commonplace, They Almost Seem Like the Truth," by Terry Lee Goodrich, *Seattle Post-Intelligencer,* October 29, 1990, C1. Reprinted courtesy of the Fort Worth Star-Telegram.

4. ___ Lying is exciting.

5. ___ Lying is dangerous.

6. ___ People should lie in order not to hurt other people's feelings.

7. ___ Lying can help us not to hurt others' feelings.

8. ___ Lying can hurt relationships.

9. ___ Lying is bad for your health.

Exercise 2

Below is a list of reasons for lying taken from the article you have just read. To make an argument stronger or clearer, authors often give specific examples. Following the list of reasons are examples of lying given in the article. Match each example with the letter of a reason given. There may be more than one possible answer, and some letters may be used more than once. Choose what you feel to be the best answer. Be prepared to defend your choice.

a. We lie to avoid doing things we should do.

b. We lie to get what we want.

c. We lie to buy time.

d. We lie to end conversations.

e. We lie because it's exciting.

f. We lie to make our stories more interesting.

g. We lie to make people agree with us.

h. We lie so as not to hurt others' feelings.

Example *d* You answer the telephone and falsely say that your newborn needs you.

1. ___ We say that we have already put a check in the mail when we haven't.

2. ___ You answer the phone and falsely say that you were just on your way out the door.

3. ___ We promise that we'll do lunch, but we never get together for lunch.

4. ___ We tell people at work that we are sick, then go out and enjoy the day.

5. ___ We tell our host that a terrible dinner was fine.

6. ___ Parents and children report different understandings of the same event.

Exercise 3

Authors of newspaper articles such as the one you just read often cite "experts," people who know a good deal about the topic the author is writing about. However, articles that mention experts can be based mostly on the personal opinion of the writer. In evaluating texts, it's important to notice whose research and opinions are being reported. Below is the list of reasons from the article for why people lie. Indicate if each one is given by the author (A) or by one of the experts (E) cited by the author.

1. ___ a. We lie to avoid doing things we should do.

   ___ b. We lie to get what we want.

   ___ c. We lie to buy time.

   ___ d. We lie to end conversations.

   ___ e. We lie because it's exciting.

   ___ f. We lie to make our stories more interesting.

   ___ g. We lie to make people agree with us.

   ___ h. We lie so as not to hurt others' feelings.

2. If you were writing a research paper on lying, would you cite this article? Why or why not?

Discussion/Composition

1. Below is a dictionary definition of *lie*.

   > ***n. a.*** a statement of something known or believed by the speaker to be untrue with the purpose of giving the hearer the wrong idea. **b.** an untrue statement that the speaker may or may not believe to be true.

   Give your definition of a lie. Explain why some things are lies and others are not.

2. Is it sometimes necessary to lie? Why or why not? Give examples from the article and from your own experience.

3. Do you think there are cultural differences in the definition of lying? Is politeness in one culture a lie in another? Use examples from the article and your own experiences to compare and contrast different ideas about lying.

Vocabulary from Context

Exercise 1

Below is the beginning of the article "Lies Are So Commonplace, They Almost Seem Like the Truth."
Use your general knowledge, your knowledge of stems and affixes, and information from the entire text
below to write a definition, synonym, or description of the italicized word on the line provided. Note
that some of the words appear more than once. Read through the entire passage before deciding on a
definition of each term. By the end of the passage, you should have a good idea of the meaning. You do
not need an exact definition; with only a general idea of the meaning, you will often be able to
understand the meaning of a written text.

Everyone *lies*. Little lies, perhaps, which may not cause serious problems, but
still they are lies. We *fudge* on how old we are, how much we weigh, what we are
paid. Some people tell their children that Santa Claus will come on Christmas Eve.

Consider the last time you got a phone call from someone you didn't want to
talk to. Did you perhaps *claim* falsely that you were just on way out the
door? That your *newborn* (you're childless) needed you?

Did you ever promise anyone, "We'll *do* lunch," when you knew that you'd
never get together?

Did you ever reach for the phone to call in sick to work, then *leap* from bed to
enjoy the day?

1. lies: _____

2. fudge: _____

3. claim: _____

4. newborn: _____

5. do: _____

6. leap: _____

Exercise 2

This exercise should be done after you have finished reading "Lies Are So Commonplace, They Almost Seem Like the Truth." The exercise will give you practice deciding on the meaning of unfamiliar words. Give a definition, synonym, or description of each of the words below. The number in parentheses indicates the paragraph in which the word can be found. Your teacher may want you to do these orally or in writing.

1. (3) behaviors: _____

2. (3) purposes: _____

3. (3) avoid: _____

4. (4) memory: _____

5. (6) destroy: _____

6. (6) trust: _____

Reading Selections 3A–3C

Popular Press

In recent years, more women have begun to work outside the home, and men seem to have taken on more tasks for families. North American magazines and newspapers have begun to write about the "new man"—whether he really exists and how changes in family life affect women. The articles and cartoons that follow are examples of these discussions from the popular press.

Selection 3A   **Popular Social Science**

For many years, Lou Harris has been questioning people in the United States about their opinions on everything from politics to love. The results of these surveys, known as the "Harris polls," have become an interesting record of popular culture. Recently, Harris published a book describing the results of a number of his surveys. The reading passage below, from a chapter in his volume *Inside America,* describes survey results on the topic of how men and women share housework. Your teacher may want you to do Vocabulary from Context exercise 1 on pages 102–3 before you begin.

Before You Begin   1. When men and women live together, do you think they should share all household tasks equally? If not, which ones should men do and which ones should women do? Why?
2. How do you think most people in the United States would answer this question?

Skimming

When an article presents a lot of statistics, it is often useful to read it first quickly to discover the organization of the article and to get a general sense of the main ideas and information presented. In this article, you will notice that the survey results are not presented in numerical tables. Skim the article first; keep in mind that your next task will be to put the statistics into tables so that they will be easier to understand.* After skimming, then, you will need to return to the article to locate the information necessary to complete the tables in Comprehension exercise 1. Your teacher may want you to do Vocabulary from Context exercise 1 before you begin.

Who's Doing the Work around the House?

1   Most adult women in the United States today work outside the home. And the majority of men and women believe that when men and women live together, household tasks should be shared by men and women. But what really happens?

Adapted from "How Nice to Have a Man Around the House—If He Shares the Chores," in *Inside America,* by Lou Harris (New York: Vintage/Random House, 1987), 98–102.
*For an introduction to skimming, see Unit 1.

2   When asked who does the household chores, 41% of all women report that they do, another 41% say they do a lot and their husbands help some, 15% report the chores being evenly divided, and 2% say the husbands do more. Clearly, there is a gap between deciding that things should be equal and the reality of who, in fact, gets things done.

3   However, it must be noted that in families where both spouses are employed, among husbands, 24% say the wife does nearly all the work around the house, 42% report that the wife does most of it but the husband helps some, 28% report that the work is evenly divided, and 5% that the husband actually does more around the house. Greater sharing within couples is also seen more among young married families under 30 years of age and among those who are college-educated.

Sharing Money

4   When both spouses work, 79% of both men and women report that both salaries are combined and used for all household expenses, personal expenses, and savings. Only 15% of husbands whose wives work say that the spouses keep their money separated after both spouses contribute a part of their salaries for household and living expenses and savings. Obviously, when it comes to money, sharing of both salaries and expenses has become the norm.

Beyond Sharing: Exchanging Roles

5   One possible way for men and women to share family responsibilities is for people to change roles: the men would stay home and the women would become the breadwinners of the family. This possibility has been surveyed since 1970. Back then, 63% said they would have less respect for a husband who stayed home than for one who had a job outside the home, only 8% would respect him more, and 15% said it would make very little difference. By 1980 things had begun to change. A much lower 41% said they would respect the stay-at-home husband less, 6% more, but 42% about the same. Now, only 25% say they would respect a man who stayed home to do household chores less, 12% more, and a big 50% say the same.

6   Thus the number who say they would think less of a husband who exchanges roles with his wife and stays home to take care of the household has declined from 63% to 25% over a generation's time. What is more, the younger people are and the more money they have, the less likely they are to say they will respect a stay-at-home husband less.

The Future: Teenagers on Sharing Chores

7   Attitudes toward change are usually formed early in life or no later than the teens. Therefore, it is significant to find that teenagers today expect to share almost all household and child-rearing chores in married life.

8   Here is what they say about sharing chores:

—On vacuuming the house, only 40% of all teenagers think this should be the responsibility of the wife, compared with 38% who say both should do it, and 20% who believe it doesn't matter who does it. The point is that a 60%–40% majority does not think it is the duty of the wife to vacuum the house.
—On mopping the house, an even 50% think that it is a woman's chore only, but an equal 50% do not think so.

—On preparing meals, 39% of the teenagers think this is a wife's responsibility, but a higher 46% see cooking as a shared future responsibility, 2% see it as primarily a man's task, and the remaining 13% say it doesn't matter.

—On washing dishes, in the past generally only a task for women, no more than 54% of teenagers believe this is a wife's task, and 46%, nearly as many, do not agree that this task should only be done by women.

—On washing the car, traditionally a man's duty, now only 40% of all teenagers think the husband should do it. Thirty-nine percent think the chore should be equally shared (49% of teenage girls feel this way), 2% think the woman should do it, and the rest say it doesn't matter.

—On mowing the lawn, almost always the man's job around the house, a large 64% still agree with tradition and say let the husband do it. But 15% of the young men and a much higher 43% of the young women simply don't agree with that. It is significant that teenage girls lead the way in feeling that many traditional men's chores should now be shared by women.

Caring for Young Children

9   On caring for young children, the teenage view is that the chores should be shared all the way:

—91% of all teenagers believe that playing with children should be an equal responsibility of husbands and wives.

—71% believe that feeding babies and young children should be a joint duty of husbands and wives.

—64% of all teens believe that changing diapers should be shared all the way, although a much higher 78% of teenage girls think this, compared with a lower 50% of teenage boys.

—87% believe that disciplining young children should be a responsibility shared between men and women.

—56% believe that bathing a baby should be the equal and joint responsibility of men and women.

—73% think that putting the baby to bed should be done just as often by husbands and wives.

—68% of all teenagers believe that putting a young child to bed must be the shared responsibility of both spouses in a good marriage.

Observation

10   It seems that the public believes it is very difficult for a young mother to work, take care of the household, and be primarily responsible for raising children. There simply is not enough time to do it all. And there is no doubt that most women in the future are going to choose to work, marry, and be mothers. Therefore, people conclude, tradition must change and male spouses must do many things that their fathers and grandfathers would not have agreed to do.

Women, especially young women, are determined to see the change come about. Even more interesting is that males, particularly teenage boys, agree with the women.

The significance of this is that right in the home, daily, the reality of equality between the sexes is being created. This newfound sharing is not simply something that people say without doing. It is a real revolution.

Comprehension

Exercise 1

Use information from "Who's Doing the Work around the House?" to complete the tables that follow.

TABLE 1.   Sharing Tasks: Reports of Who Does Household Chores (%)

Who Does Chores	Family Arrangement	
	All Families (Women's reports)	Families in Which Both Spouses Work (Men's reports)
Women do nearly all		
Women do most; husbands help		
Task evenly divided		
Husbands do more		

TABLE 2.   Sharing Money: Men's and Women's Reports When Both Work (%)

Salaries combined for all things	
Some money kept separately	

TABLE 3.   Exchanging Roles: Respect for Stay-At-Home Husbands (%)

Respect for the husband	Year		
	1970	1980	Now
Would respect him less			
Would respect him more			
Would respect him the same			

TABLE 4.   Teenagers Sharing Chores (%)

Who Does Chore	Chore					
	Vacuum	Mop	Cook	Wash Dishes	Wash Car	Mow Lawn
Women's work						✕
Shared work						
Men's work						
Doesn't matter who does it						✕

Exercise 2

Answer the following questions based on your understanding of the passage and the tables you have completed in Comprehension exercise 1.

1. T / F   Based on the Harris Poll, women do most of the housework.

2. T / F   When both men and women work, they say they typically share their salaries and expenses.

3. T / F   Today, most people in the United States have less respect for a stay-at-home husband than for a "working" husband.

4. T / F   Teenagers believe there are no household tasks that should be done only by women.

5. T / F   Most teenagers believe that caring for young children should be shared by men and women.

Discussion/Composition

1. These survey results are based on what people say they do or say they believe. How believable do you find these self-reports? Support your opinion with information from your reading or from your personal experience.

2. The author says that based on the teenagers' beliefs about the future, "a real revolution" is happening in U.S. homes. Do you agree? Use information from the article and your own observations about life.

3. The teenagers surveyed hope that they will be able to avoid traditional patterns around the house. But is this possible? On page 102 is a cartoon from the comic strip "Sally Forth." Sally and her husband Ted are a modern couple who both have careers outside the home. They work hard on their

marriage and friendship. It's not always easy to be a "modern couple." But when they have problems, they are able to face these with humor.

In this cartoon, Sally's and Ted's daughter is asking how they decided who would do which tasks in the house. How does Sally feel about this? How does Ted feel? Explain the world from either Sally's or Ted's point of view.

Reprinted with special permission of King Features Syndicate.

4. When men and women live together, should they share all household tasks? Support your opinion with information from the article and your own observations.

5. Using the information in the article and the tables, summarize the major findings in this article. Be sure to compare and contrast different groups and time periods.

Vocabulary from Context

Exercise 1

Both the ideas and the vocabulary in the exercise below are taken from "Who's Doing the Work around the House?" Use the context provided to decide on meanings for the italicized words. Write a definition, synonym, or description in the space provided.

1. _____

2. _____

3. _____

4. _____

Much has been written of late about the sharing of household tasks between men and women. *Chores* once thought to belong only to one sex, for example, fixing cars by men and cooking by women, are now shared—at least by some. But there is a *gap* between what people say should happen and what they actually do. Although most people think chores should be shared, many report this is not what happens. However, some couples are better at sharing the money they earn. Their *salaries* are combined and this is used to pay for all household *expenses,* such as the bills for food, light, and housing.

5. _____   One way of sharing tasks is for men and women to change *roles:* men
would do traditional women's jobs, and women would become the
6. _____   breadwinners. People tend to have strong feelings about this. *Attitudes*
toward this possibility have been surveyed for about 30 years. People
have been asked whether they would have a lower opinion of a stay-
at-home husband than of a man who is employed outside the home. A
7. _____   *generation* ago, when the parents of today's adults were asked, they
8. _____   said they would *have less respect for* men who switched roles.

Today's teenagers have different views about most things. For
9. _____   example, they no longer think that *child-rearing* is the job only of a
10. _____   mother. They believe the *responsibility* for taking care of children
should be shared. Similarly, they no longer believe that correcting or
punishing children who misbehave is the job only of a father. Most
11. _____   believe the *disciplining* of children should be shared.

Exercise 2

*This exercise gives you additional clues to the meaning of unfamiliar vocabulary in context. In the
paragraph of "Who's Doing the Work around the House?" indicated by the number in parentheses, find
the word or phrase that best fits the meaning given. Your teacher may want to read these aloud as you
quickly scan the paragraph to find the answer.*

1.   (4) What word means *money put away for the future?*

2.   (4) What phrase means *typical; average; what most people do?*

3.   (5) What word means *people who bring home the money,* that is, *who buy the bread?*

4.   (6) What word means *probable?*

5.   (8) What word means *responsibility; task; job?*

6.   (8) What word means *mostly; mainly?*

7. (10) What phrase means *want very much; have made a decision?*

8. (10) What word means *importance?*

9. (10) What word means *new; newly discovered?*

 Selection 3B   **Cartoons**

Before You Begin   1. What do you think would happen if a married couple exchanged household
tasks for a day? Do you think each of them might learn something?
2. What are things that women do around the house that men might not notice?
What things that men do might go unnoticed by women?

The cartoons that follow are taken from the comic strip "Sally Forth." Sally and Ted are a "modern couple" who both have careers outside the home. When they have problems, they try to face these with humor. The comic strips were printed over the course of a week in newspapers throughout North America. Read each strip only for the main idea and the humor, then answer the questions that follow.

Sally Forth

Monday:

1. Why are Sally and Ted going to switch roles for a week?

2. When Ted and Sally switch roles, what is the first job Ted will do? What will Sally do?

Tuesday:

1. What is Ted's household task in today's cartoon?

2. Why does Ted want their daughter to wait until next week to get sick?

Wednesday:

Reprinted with special permission of King Features Syndicate.

1. What is Ted's task today?

2. The cartoonist says that Sally and Ted are reversing roles. What has been reversed in Wednesday's comic strip?

Thursday:

Reprinted with special permission of King Features Syndicate.

1. What is Ted's task today?

2. What does his daughter mean when she says, "It's working"?

Friday:

SALLY FORTH By Greg Howard

Reprinted with special permission of King Features Syndicate.

1. Was the week of switching roles successful?

2. Why does Sally want to kick Ted?

Discussion/Composition

1. We know what tasks Ted did during this week of switching roles. What do you think Sally was doing? Whose role would you want? Why?

2. Think of a household you are familiar with in which a man and a woman could switch roles for a week. What do you think would happen? Be sure to give specific examples.

3. Humor grows from the culture in which it occurs. Did you find this series of cartoons funny? Do you think these cartoon strips would seem funny in your community/country? Why or why not?

Selection 3C   **Magazine Article**

Before You Begin   1. What do you think makes a good father?

   2. Are there reasons why some women might not want men to be more active in raising children and taking care of a home?

The magazine article you are about to read argues that there is no single way to be a good father and discusses reasons why all men are not "new fathers." Your teacher may want you to do the Vocabulary from Context exercise 1 on page 110 before you begin reading.

The "New Father"
No Real Role Reversal

1   Although we hear much about the "new father," the man who takes an active role in the day-to-day care of his children, there is no single way to be a good father, claims Michael Lamb, a psychologist with the National Institute of Child Health and Human Development. He says children can do very well in many different situations, and the greater involvement of fathers is probably most important when it makes mothers' lives happier.

2   In the U.S., about half the men questioned reply that if there were no job-related penalty, they would like to spend more time with their children. Looked at another way, the other 50% are satisfied the way things are and are saying that they don't feel any great desire to spend more time with their children than they currently do. The same questionnaires often ask women if they are satisfied with the amount of their husbands' participation in child-rearing. Thirty-five to forty percent say they would like their partners to do more.

3   What is often overlooked, Lamb says, is that about two thirds of the women are happy with their spouses' current level of parental involvement. "The truth is that men are not asking to be more involved with the children, but women are not trying to get them more involved, either. For many reasons, both men and women, on average, are more or less satisfied with traditional responsibilities." The fact that women don't necessarily want men to have more involvement in child-rearing "has a lot to do with power and privilege in this society. Women fear they may lose power and status in the family, which is the one area in which these had never been questioned. At the same time, they do not have equality in the world of work. For many women, it's better to keep their responsibility for parenthood, even if that means they have what might be called role overload, rather than give some of that status, responsibility, and power to a partner."

4   Fathers often say they aren't more active parents because they don't have child-caring skills. "But women are just as frightened by parenthood and just as poorly prepared as men. The difference is that they're expected to know how to do it. From the time the baby is born, everybody acts as if either they know or they better find out fast because no one else is going to do it." If the same thing were expected of men, they, too, would learn. "All the evidence we have suggests that when fathers try caring for children, they can do it just as well as mothers can, with the exception of making milk."

5   What is important, notes Lamb, is that parents be able to divide child care responsibilities in a way that suits their individual needs. If the father doesn't want to be involved and a traditional mother agrees, those children would be better off if the father were not highly involved because that would make everyone more comfortable. It is not better to have a father stay home who doesn't want to be there. "Father involvement has to be looked at in the context of the family arrangements and the value it has for both mothers and fathers."

Adapted from "The 'New Father': No Real Role Reversal," *USA Today,* July, 1989, 11.

Comprehension

Answer the following questions according to your understanding of the passage. Indicate if statements 1–4 are true (T) or false (F).

1. T / F   Most married mothers would be happier if their husbands were more involved in caring for the children.

2. T / F   Most married mothers are happy with their husband's current level of involvement with the children.

3. T / F   Work in the home gives a person no power or status in the United States.

4. T / F   In the United States, women are better prepared to be parents than are men.

5. If a father doesn't want to be involved in caring for his children and the mother wants him to be, what would the author of the article think would be best for the children?

Discussion/Composition

1. The author states that fathers care for children just as well as mothers do. Do you agree? Use examples from reading you have done on this topic and personal experience to support your opinion.

2. The author of this article believes that no single style of family is best for children. Do you agree? Do you think that some "family arrangements" (that is, who does what in the family) are not good for children? Use examples from reading you have done on this topic and personal experience to support your opinion.

3. a. Do people feel the same way about "new fathers" and "new mothers"? On page 109 is a cartoon showing some business people's feelings about "a new kind of father." How do their reactions to the father and mother differ?

   b. Compare difficulties in the workplace faced by working women and by "new fathers." Use information from your discussion of this cartoon and your own knowledge.

4. People in many countries feel that family life is different today than it was in the past. Penelope Leach, author of the popular parenting book *Your Baby and Child,* believes that things do feel different, but she argues that the causes of these feelings are not what we think. According to Leach, what has changed is not that more women have begun to work, but that the *place* where everyone works has changed. Here is a summary of Leach's beliefs from *Time* magazine:

> The change, according to Penelope Leach, comes from the Industrial Revolution, which forced a separation between home and the work place. "Home and its surrounding community used to be the central place where everyone spent the day, with work and play and family pretty much intermixed," she says. "Now work has moved into geographically separate production centers and takes the form of specialized jobs that cannot be shared or done with a baby on your back." Home has become a place where people do little more than sleep, get cleaned up, and change clothes. And as mothers have increasingly left home for the office or factory, children's separation from the adult world has very much increased.

Summarize Leach's views in two or three sentences. Then indicate whether you think her argument is a strong one. Be sure to support your opinion.

Cartoon from *Z Magazine,* July/August 1994, 31.
Paragraph adapted from "The Great Experiment," *Time* (Special Issue), Fall 1990, 74.

Vocabulary from Context

Exercise 1

Both the ideas and the vocabulary in the exercise below are taken from "The 'New Father': No Real Role Reversal." Use the context provided to decide on meanings for the italicized words. Some of these words are also taught with Selection 3A. Write a definition, synonym, or description in the space provided.

1. _____

2. _____

3. _____

4. _____

Much has been written about the so-called new father, the man who takes an active part in taking care of his children. This *involvement* by fathers in *child-rearing* has been shown in questionnaires given to men and women about their participation in child-rearing. The questionnaires show that some men are taking more *responsibility* for their children. But also, many women are still doing more than men in the home even though they are working outside the home. This means that women have two *roles:* the role of parent and of worker. And the heavy responsibilities of both these roles make women very tired.

5. _____

6. _____

This role overload can be explained in part by the fact that not all women want their male spouses to be more involved in child care. Raising children has traditionally been the place where women get power and *status*. Their position in society has come from their role as mothers. And this role has given them the *privilege* to have things their way in the home. It is hard to give up this status and privilege, to let men take over in the home, when women are still not equal in the workplace.

7. _____

8. _____

And not all men want to be more involved at home. Even if this involvement would not hurt men's careers, many say they would not want to be more involved at home. That is, even if there is no job-related *penalty* at work, many men like things the way they are. The *arrangements* whereby family roles and tasks are divided are difficult to change.

Exercise 2

This exercise gives you additional clues to the meaning of unfamiliar vocabulary in context. In the paragraph of "The 'New Father'" indicated by the number in parentheses, find the word that best fits the meaning given. Your teacher may want to read these aloud as you quickly scan the paragraph to find the answer.

1. (2) Which word means *happy; pleased?*

2. (2) Which word means *involvement; taking part?*

3. (3) Which word means *looked past; not noticed; missed; ignored?*

4. (4) Which word means *child-rearing?*

5. (5) Which word means *fits; agrees with; satisfies?*

Reading Selection 4

Magazine Graphic

The maps and charts on the following pages contain information published in *Time* magazine. They provide readers with a picture of problems facing the world. Your teacher may want you to do Vocabulary from Context exercise 1 on pages 120–21 before you begin.

  The article presents the information in two ways. Some of the information appears in maps and report cards (pages 115 and 117) that grade selected countries on their efforts to solve environmental problems. Information about problems facing individual countries is presented in brief reports (pages 118–19).

Before You Begin   1. Which parts of the world are you interested in reading about?

  2. What sorts of environmental problems do you expect to read about?

Summit to Save the Earth: The World's Next Trouble Spots

with report cards for major countries on . . .

Air Pollution	Population Growth	Safe Drinking Water	Protected Lands

  What kind of world will our children have to live in? Will they have air to breathe and food to eat? These are among the basic questions that were addressed at the first world meeting on the environment, attended by more than 100 world leaders and 30,000 other scientists, newspeople, and concerned citizens. These complex problems can no longer be solved by individual countries; nations of the world must act together if we are to develop answers that will give a safe and healthy world to our children. Will world leaders have the vision to make the necessary changes in the laws that protect the environment? The answer is not certain, but there is hope.

  A number of important problems were examined in the summit conference, all related to quality of life on the planet. As more and more countries become industrialized, air pollution from factories and automobiles worsens, causing an increase in disease and medical costs. Many leaders are concerned about birth rates because the populations of their countries are growing faster than their economies. Clean water is, of course, another concern for all countries, but very

Adapted from *Time,* June 1, 1992, 64–65. © 1992 Time, Inc. Reprinted by permission.

often rivers and other water sources are threatened by industrial growth, as factories and other large businesses look for ways to dispose of chemical waste matter. Another area where industry and nature must be balanced is in the use of forests, jungles, grasslands, and deserts; government officials argue that the land is needed for farming, industry, and housing, while environmentalists say that we need to preserve the wild lands.

Environmentalists have "graded" the world on environmental problems. They have provided the "report cards" that appear with the maps. Like the report cards that teachers send home with school children, these give us a better understanding of how we are doing in taking care of the Earth.

Getting Oriented

Study the maps and the report cards on the following pages to understand how the information is organized, then answer the questions below.

1. What are the four environmental problems on which the countries are graded? _____

   _____

2. How have the countries of the world been grouped for evaluation? _____

   _____

Grading the World

Within each geographical area several countries have been given grades on each of the four environmental problems. The grades are explained in the Key to Report Cards box. Take a few minutes to study the report cards and the key, then answer the questions below. The questions require you to use the maps and report cards. Some may require that you look at the brief reports on pages 118–19. True/False items are indicated by a T / F before a statement. Some questions may have more than one correct answer. Others may require an opinion. Choose the answer you like best; be prepared to defend your choices. Your teacher may want you to work individually, in pairs, or in small groups.

1. Look at the Key to Report Cards.

   a. Notice that air pollution is graded according to "per capita CO_2 emissions".* This means the amount of carbon dioxide in the air compared with the number of people who live in the area. Would you want to live in a country with high CO_2 emissions? Why or why not?

   _____

   b. T / F   Population growth is measured by counting the number of babies born every year.

   c. Areas are graded according to the percentage of the country that is protected. What do you think this means? Protected against what?

   _____

   d. Before looking at the maps, predict the grades that you believe your own area of the world would receive.

   _____

2. T / F   The U.S. has no serious environmental problems.

3. Based on the information provided above, would you rather live in Argentina or Mexico? Why?

   _____

4. T / F   Building the dam in Costa Rica will give jobs to 3,000 Indians.

5. T / F   The tourist industry is not all good for Belize.

6. T / F   The land along the Bio-Bio River in Chile is not liveable.

7. For which two countries in South America is oil a problem? _____

---

*CO_2 is the chemical formula for carbon dioxide. Carbon monoxide (CO) is a deadly gas that comes primarily from automobiles.

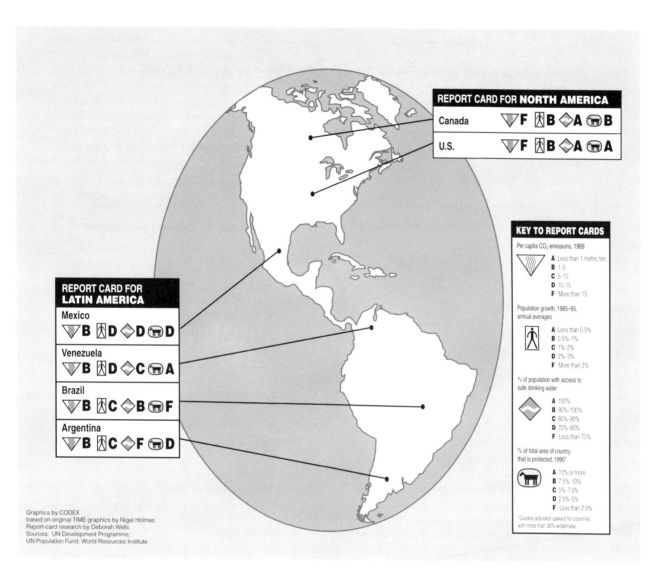

REPORT CARD FOR NORTH AMERICA

Canada	🔻	F	🚶	B	◇	A	🐂	B
U.S.	🔻	F	🚶	B	◇	A	🐂	A

REPORT CARD FOR LATIN AMERICA

Mexico
🔻 B 🚶 D ◇ D 🐂 D

Venezuela
🔻 B 🚶 D ◇ C 🐂 A

Brazil
🔻 B 🚶 C ◇ B 🐂 F

Argentina
🔻 B 🚶 C ◇ F 🐂 D

KEY TO REPORT CARDS

Per capita CO_2 emissions, 1989

A Less than 1 metric ton
B 1–5
C 5–10
D 10–15
F More than 15

Population growth, 1985–95, annual averages

A Less than 0.5%
B 0.5%–1%
C 1%–2%
D 2%–3%
F More than 3%

% of population with access to safe drinking water

A 100%
B 90%–100%
C 80%–90%
D 70%–80%
F Less than 70%

% of total area of country that is protected, 1990*

A 10% or more
B 7.5%–10%
C 5%–7.5%
D 2.5%–5%
F Less than 2.5%

*Grades adjusted upward for countries with more than 30% wilderness.

Graphics by CODEX
based on original TIME graphics by Nigel Holmes
Report-card research by Deborah Wells
Sources: UN Development Programme;
UN Population Fund; World Resources Institute

8. Find your own area of the world. What grades did your area receive? Do you agree with the evaluation? Why or why not?

_____

9. Which of the four environmental problems do you worry about the most? Why? _____

_____

10. Which environmental problem appears to be the most serious for countries throughout the world? (Another way to think about this question is to ask yourself which environmental problem received the most F's?)

_____

11. Which countries have the most serious problems with CO_2 emissions? _____

12. T / F   Europe's air is generally cleaner than that of Latin America.

13. Based on the information in the report cards, would you rather live in Spain or Germany? Why?

_____

Reporting on the World

Skim and scan the brief reports (pages 118–19) for answers to the following questions.*

1. T / F   Skiers have damaged the Alps.

2. T / F   Bulgaria uses nuclear power to meet the country's energy needs.

3. In many countries, meeting basic needs today (for food and fuel, for example) makes it difficult to plan for the future. Botswana, Ethiopia, and Madagascar are examples.

   a. T / F   In Botswana, the government is working to provide drinking water for the growing population.

   b. T / F   In Ethiopia, more food today may mean less food tomorrow.

   c. T / F   In 35 years, Madagascar will have no forests.

4. Why are Australia's desert bandicoot and lesser bilby extinct? _____

5. T / F   In Nepal, the problem of trash along mountain trails has been solved.

6. T / F   It is possible to do this exercise without becoming sad or angry.

_____

*For an introduction to skimming and scanning, see Unit 1.

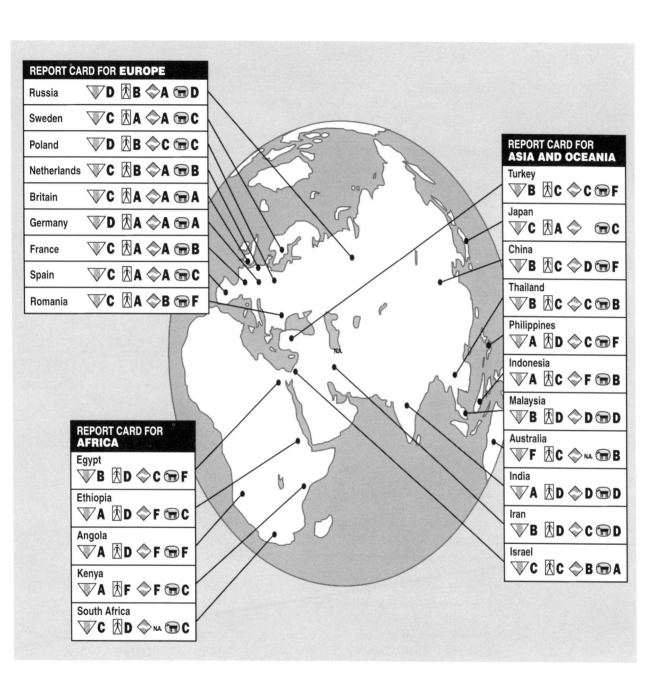

REPORT CARD FOR EUROPE

Russia	▽D	☖B	◇A	⛫D
Sweden	▽C	☖A	◇A	⛫C
Poland	▽D	☖B	◇C	⛫C
Netherlands	▽C	☖B	◇A	⛫B
Britain	▽C	☖A	◇A	⛫A
Germany	▽D	☖A	◇A	⛫A
France	▽C	☖A	◇A	⛫B
Spain	▽C	☖A	◇A	⛫C
Romania	▽C	☖A	◇B	⛫F

REPORT CARD FOR ASIA AND OCEANIA

Turkey	▽B	☖C	◇C	⛫F
Japan	▽C	☖A	◇	⛫C
China	▽B	☖C	◇D	⛫F
Thailand	▽B	☖C	◇C	⛫B
Philippines	▽A	☖D	◇C	⛫F
Indonesia	▽A	☖C	◇F	⛫B
Malaysia	▽B	☖D	◇D	⛫D
Australia	▽F	☖C	◇N.A.	⛫B
India	▽A	☖D	◇D	⛫D
Iran	▽B	☖D	◇C	⛫D
Israel	▽C	☖C	◇B	⛫A

REPORT CARD FOR AFRICA

Egypt	▽B	☖D	◇C	⛫F
Ethiopia	▽A	☖D	◇F	⛫C
Angola	▽A	☖D	◇F	⛫F
Kenya	▽A	☖F	◇F	⛫C
South Africa	▽C	☖D	◇N.A.	⛫C

Brief Reports

1   **British Columbia.** The timber industry has clear-cut more than half of the trees on Vancouver Island, and in the next 25 years the rest could be gone.

2   **United States.** The Florida Keys, a marine sanctuary, is dying at the rate of 4% to 10% a year. Pollution from farming and warmer water temperatures is the major problem.

3   **Belize.** This small country's growing tourist industry could harm the coast. Fish and other wildlife, as well as the fragile reef,* are threatened by large numbers of swimmers and pollution from hotels.

4   **Ecuador.** Ecuador's large Cuyabeno National Park provides a safe environment for a wide variety of animals such as pink dolphins, harpy eagles, and jaguars. But the park is endangered by the construction of oil wells and new roads and by the increased use of land for farming.

5   **Costa Rica.** The government wants to dam the Pacuara River for a hydroelectric plant because Costa Rica needs more energy. But the project would flood 3,000 acres of forest and displace numerous groups of Indians.

6   **Chile.** Five new power stations are planned for the Bio-Bio River, as well as a large dam that will flood nearly 11,860 acres of land. Environmentalists say that the land along the river could become unfit for living.

7   **Argentina.** Oil leaks from ships carrying oil off the coast of Patagonia have caused major damage to the marine life. Hunting threatens many rare types of animals.

8   **Poland.** The Dunajac valley is famous for its scenery and castles. A dam will soon be completed on the river, however, that will destroy important natural preserves.†

9   **The Alps.** These famous mountains are scarred by roads, railways, and ski runs. Native plants are dying, the air is polluted, and mudslides are common.

10 **Bulgaria.** The nuclear power plant at Kozlodoy has been called, "the most dangerous in the world." It has had numerous problems with leaks, fires, and failures. The cost for fixing the plant will be over $1 billion, but it supplies 40% of the country's energy needs, so it must be kept running.

11 **Black Sea.** The Sea is fed by some of the most polluted rivers in the world, and large numbers of fish and animals are disappearing from its shores and waters.

12 **Siberia.** Nearly twice the size of the Amazon jungle, Siberia's forests contain about 25% of the world's wood. Government planners hope to increase the amount of lumber sold to foreign governments. Environmentalists fear that this will result in erosion of land that will pollute the rivers.

13 **Botswana.** The large Oksvango River delta‡ provides homes for some of Africa's last wild herds of elephant, Cape buffalo, and zebra. But the area could be hurt by a plan to clean out 23 miles of river to provide drinking water for growing towns. Environmentalists who are against the project say the project is really meant to help the country's diamond mining industry.

Reefs are rocklike underwater structures that provide homes and food for fish and other forms of wildlife.

†*Preserves* are areas of land or water where animals and vegetation are protected from problems caused by human activity.

‡A *delta* is the broad, flat land area formed over the years at the mouth of a river; it is very rich in vegetation and animal life.

14   **Ethiopia.** For over one hundred years, the growing population of Ethiopia has cut more than 90% of the country's forests for firewood and farmland, allowing 1 billion tons of valuable earth to erode into the sea. As a result, some 8,000 acres of farmland can no longer produce food.

15   **Madagascar.** Madagascar is populated by at least 150,000 species of plants and animals found nowhere else in the world. However, 80% of the island's forests has been cut for farming and fuel. If this continues, Madagascar will have no forests in 35 years.

16   **Persian Gulf.** About 8 million barrels of oil have been dumped into the Gulf in recent years, in some cases completely covering areas where animals and birds live.

17   **India.** The $10 billion Namada Valley Development Plan will include more than 3,000 dams, displace as many as 100,000 people, submerge forests and farms, and increase the river's salt levels and mud content.

18   **Malaysia.** If the rate of logging continues, Malaysia's forests will disappear in about ten years.

19   **Indonesia.** Over 2.2 million acres of tropical forest are cut every year here for wood products. In Kalimantan province, fires, logging, and coal mining have destroyed so much forest that environmentalists say all is lost.

20   **Australia.** Miners, loggers, and tourists have damaged the Tasmanian Tarkine Wilderness area, adding to problems caused by years of overgrazing of cattle and sheep. At least half of the region's animals have become extinct, including the desert bandicoot and the lesser bilby.

21   **Johnston Atoll.** This tiny island 700 miles west of Hawaii is a U.S. national wildlife area. It is also the site of a $240 million toxic waste disposal system that threatens the health of the area.

22   **China.** A proposed dam on the Yangtze River will take 18 years to build and could provide China with 17,680 megawatts of power. However, the dam could cost $29 billion, and more than 1 million people will be displaced.

23   **Nepal.** Foreigners have long left trash along the trails that lead to the world's highest mountains. The government can do little to stop this, and several international environmental groups have begun a yearly effort to clean up the area.

Discussion/Composition

1. Why should people be concerned about the loss of forests in countries far from their own?

2. What would you say is the most serious cause of environmental problems? Support your answer with examples from your reading and your personal experience.

3. The brief reports describe a problem faced by both India and China. What is it? What are their choices? What would you recommend they do?

4. What do you think you and other individuals might do to help solve these problems? Choose an area of the world where you have experience, and give examples of things you might do.

Vocabulary from Context

Exercise 1

Both the vocabulary and the ideas in the exercise below are taken from "Summit to Save the Earth."
Use the context provided to decide on meanings for the italicized words. Write a definition, synonym, or
description in the space provided.

1. _____ It has been known for some time that *population* growth is a serious problem. As the number of people in the world increases, the need for food, water, and homes also increases.

2. _____ People from around the world recently met to discuss serious *environmental* problems such as dirty air and water, overpopulation, and the effect on nature of growing cities.

3. _____ *Summits,* meetings which bring together leaders from important countries, are often the only way to solve such complex problems.

4. _____ When *industrialization* first began in the early 1900s, few people questioned the value of using machines to do the work commonly done by humans.

5. _____
6. _____ The growing *economies* that provided jobs and produced goods for people to buy also *polluted* the air and the water supplies near the cities. Factories filled the air with smoke while at the same time they sent waste products into the rivers and streams.

7. _____ Many of the chemical by-products of modern farm and factory processes are *toxic.* Because they kill animals and plants, it is important to dispose of them properly so that they do not harm forests, rivers, or farmland.

8. _____ Factories and farms produce *chemical waste.* Because the chemicals cannot be used, they are often just washed into open fields and rivers, creating toxic conditions for plants and animals.

9. _____ When power and water was needed by the growing cities, people *dammed* the rivers around the world. The lakes that resulted often destroyed land used for crops and forced people to move from their farms.

10. _____
11. _____ When *lumber* was needed to build houses, people cut down trees. The population increased and more *timber* was needed to build houses. Serious problems began to develop. Very often the lumber companies
12. _____ *clear-cut* the forests, removing all the trees and leaving the land bare.
13. _____ When the rains came, the earth was washed away. This *erosion* of rich earth left land where no food could grow.

14. _____

15. _____

16. _____

Unfortunately, most of us did not realize the damage that our growing cities were causing. The *rate* of growth was so fast, and the needs of industrialized countries so great, that we did not stop to ask ourselves what was being *threatened* by these efforts. In fact, our behavior endangered forests and animals. We often chose to ignore the fact that our growing cities *displaced* birds and animals, who had to move away from humans.

17. _____

Humans have developed many ways to hurt the environment. *Damage* can be caused by farming, by industrial development, and by hunting and fishing.

18. _____
19. _____

Another serious environmental problem comes from *trash.* Hikers and tourists often throw cans and paper away instead of *disposing* of the trash in trash cans.

20. _____

There is a *balance* in nature that can be hurt by the smallest change in living conditions. For example, in a healthy environment, the amount of plant food is just right for the number of fish in a river; however, when the river is dammed, the balance changes. Too many fish or too much plant life can make the river unliveable.

Many countries have passed laws to protect the environment; these include such things as requiring factories and automobiles to reduce pollution and limiting the numbers of animals that can be killed by

21. _____

hunters.

22. _____

In their efforts to protect the environment, governments are often forced to choose between farm animals and *wild* animals. This is because land which has been cleared for farm animals is unhealthy for animals living outside human control.

23. _____

Increasingly, people are cutting down forests in *tropical* areas of the world, where the hot temperatures and large amounts of rainfall produce fast-growing timber.

24. _____

25. _____
26. _____

27. _____

Some types of animals (the jaguar, for example) have been killed off to the point that very few still exist. A number of these *rare* animals live in areas where new dams are planned. In many cases, they could become *extinct.* It would be sad if we lost these animals forever. For this reason, environmentalists work to *protect* animals so that they can reproduce until their numbers increase to a safe level. One solution is to create *preserves,* large areas of land or water where animals and fish are protected.

28. _____

Most people would want to protect their *quality of life,* for example, good jobs and comfortable homes in clean cities. But environmentalists point out that the first step in protecting our quality of life is protecting our environment.

Exercise 2

This exercise gives you additional clues to the meaning of unfamiliar vocabulary in context. In the brief report indicated in parentheses, find the word or phrase that best fits the meaning given. Your teacher may want to read these aloud as you quickly scan the text to find the answer.

1. (United States) What phrase means *a safe place for sea animals and plants?*

2. (Belize)   What word means *delicate; easily damaged?*

3. (The Alps)   What word means *damaged; hurt?*

4. (Australia)   What word means *to eat the grass down to the roots; to hurt the land by overeating?*

Appendix

Below is a list of the stems and affixes that appear in *Choice Readings, International Edition: Book 1.* The number in parentheses indicates the unit in which the item appears.

Prefixes

(1) **bi-**   two

(3) **de-**   away, down, reverse the action of

(3) **e-, ex-**   out, away

(3) **in-, im-**   in, into, on

(1) **mono-**   one

(1) **multi-**   many

(1) **poly-**   many

(3) **pre-**   before

(3) **re-, retro-**   again, back

(1) **semi-**   half

(3) **tele-**   far, distant

(3) **trans-**   across

(1) **tri-**   three

(1) **uni-**   one

Stems

(3) **-audi-, -audit-**   hear

(3) **-dic-, -dict-**   say, speak

(3) **-fact-, -fect-, -fic-**   make, do

(3) **-graph-, -gram-**   write, writing

(3) **-mit-, -miss-**   send

(3) **-pon-, -pos-**   put, place

(3) **-port-**   carry

(3) **-scrib-, -script-**   write

(3) **-spect-**   look

(3) **-vid-, -vis-**   see

(3) **-voc-, -vok-**   call

Suffixes

(3) **-able, -ible, -ble**   (adj.) capable of, fit for

(3) **-er, -or**   (noun) one who

(3) **-ion, -tion**   (noun) state, condition, the act of

(3) **-ize**   (verb) to make, to become

Answer Key

The processes involved in arriving at an answer are often more important than the answer itself. It is expected that students will not use the Answer Key until they have completed the exercises and are prepared to defend their answers. If a student's answer does not agree with the Key, it is important for the student to return to the exercise to discover the reason why. In some cases, no answer is provided. This is because the students have been asked to express their own opinion. In other cases, the answer provided by the authors invites more discussion and thought by students. Teachers should look upon the Answer Key as another opportunity to engage students in meaningful interaction.

Unit 1

Discourse Focus: Reading for Different Goals

Skimming (pages 1–2)
1. This page provides information about entertainment possibilities for the weekend; it is organized by day.
2. It lists times, places, and descriptions of events. Your reaction to this page will depend on your interests.
3. No. Information on renting an apartment will be found in the classified advertisements.
4. It depends on when your friends have dinner, but you could go to the auto exhibit (9 A.M.–4 P.M.) or you could do some origami at 3 P.M. or you could listen to the Colorado Honor Band at 2:30 P.M.

Scanning (page 2)
1. Jazz: Friday and Saturday Eddie Daniels will be playing with the Colorado Symphony Orchestra, Boettcher Concert Hall at 8 P.M.; tickets cost from $8.00 to $26.00. Saturday the Ron Miles Trio Plus will perform at the New Dance Theatre of Cleo Parker Robinson at 8:30 P.M.; tickets are $10.00, $8.00 for students.
2. Auto exhibit: True; Sunday, 9 A.M. to 4 P.M. at University Hills Mall, $5.00.
3. Friday night; Red Rocks Amphitheatre; 7:30 P.M.; $19.50.

Thorough Comprehension (page 3)
1. At the Denver Auditorium Theatre
2. F   3. T   4. F

Critical Reading (pages 3–5)
1. Jazz seems to be popular, as are outdoor events and informal gatherings. What do you think?
2. F (Bluegrass is a type of music.)
3. F
4. a. a variety of classical and popular songs
   b. T (But if you want to give some money, it won't be refused.)
   c. T or F, depending on you and your new friends. What do you think?
5. Origami is the age-old art of Japanese paper folding. In a workshop, you learn by doing.
6. Answers will vary according to your interests.

Nonprose Reading: Airline Terminal Maps

Part 1: Getting Oriented (page 6)
1. This depends on you. Possible answers include: Use the rest room, change a ticket, find flight information, get your luggage, go shopping.
2. No rest rooms are shown on the map.
3. At JFK, Customs and Immigration is located in terminal 4A, in the center of gates 21–32. At Atlanta, Immigration is located in the North Terminal, near the International Concourse.
4. In JFK, there are two baggage claim areas; in terminal 4B, the baggage claim area is located in the lower level, and in terminal 4A, the baggage claim area is located near the street, next to the Ambassadors Club.

Part 2: JFK International Airport (pages 6–7)
5. Flights within the U.S. (domestic flights) usually leave from terminal 4B. To get there from terminal 4A, you can take the shuttle bus from gate 21 to gate 17, or you could leave terminal 4A, turn right and walk to terminal 4B.
6. The map does not say exactly where to catch the bus or taxi. You could ask a TWA employee, or you could just walk outside to find the taxi stands or bus stops.

Part 3: Atlanta International Airport (pages 7–8)
7. According to the map, the terminal does not appear to be too far from the gates, but you might want to ask someone who knows the airport.
8. The closest place would be the "Ticketing Station" located just between the terminal and the concourses, or you could go to "Ticketing," in the North Terminal.
9. F. Baggage claim for TWA is located in the North Terminal.
10. F. All "public ground transportation" (e.g., taxis and buses) is available just outside the terminal on the west end.
11. This item is intended for discussion; the answer depends on your opinion. (But we like Atlanta better than JFK.)

Word Study: Context Clues

Exercise 1 (pages 11–12)

1. perched: sat upon
2. adopt: to take someone into a family, especially used when children become legal members of a family that is not their biological family
3. tusks: long teeth that stick out of the elephant's mouth
4. railing: shouting and complaining and arguing
5. slithered: to move like a snake
6. poking: to push with a pointed object
7. periodontist: a kind of dentist, a dentist who specializes in gums
8. taciturn: quiet; serious
9. ravenous: extremely hungry
10. curb: reduce; control

Word Study: Stems and Affixes

Exercise 1 (pages 13–16)

1. bilingual, trilingual or multilingual
2. c, a, b
3. a.

   b.

4. polygamy: having two or more marriage partners at one time (What is bigamy?)
5. automobile, television, sister, computer, woman, syllable
6. a
7. Here is one kind of triangl ◿ . Triangles have three angles.
8. b
9. Semiskilled workers use the simpler machines.
10. semiprivate rooms: rooms with two or three patients
11. multicultural: concerning many cultures
12. multiracial: concerning many races
13. triplets: three children born to the same mother at one time
14. uniform: one form; having the same clothing
15. Multimillionaires have more than one million dollars (but that doesn't mean *you* would be happy with all that money).
16. 1976
17. multicolored: having many colors
18. tripod: a stand with three legs (feet) used by photographers to hold their cameras still
19. b

Exercise 2 (pages 16–17)

1. semiannually: twice a year (at the halfway points in the year)
2. multipurpose: having many purposes
3. monocle: an eyeglass for one eye
4. triple: increase by three times
5. unification: bringing together; making one
6. monotone: a sound with only one tone
7. semifinal: in a competition, the event that determines who will play for the championship; the game before the final game
8. bilateral: agreed to by two sides
9. multistory: having many floors
10. semidarkness: partial darkness; the theatre is almost completely dark

Sentence Study: Comprehension (pages 21–23)

1. c	3. d	5. d	7. a	9. b
2. a	4. a	6. b	8. a	10. c

Paragraph Reading: Main Idea (pages 25–29)

1. c	4. d	7. d
2. d	5. c	8. a
3. b	6. b	9. c

Unit 2

Reading Selection 1: Newspaper Article
"Is McDonald's Fair?"

Comprehension (page 31)

1. a fast-food restaurant
2. T
3. T
4. 13%
5. $5.00
6. T
7. F
8. Slaves were not paid for their work, and Edward believed that he was not paid enough for his work.
9. T

Vocabulary from Context

Exercise 1 (page 32)

1. exploited: treated unfairly; in a position that you have no choice
2. slave labor: work without pay and done against one's will; slaves are people who are sold to work for others. They earn nothing except food and a place to sleep.
3. fired: forced to leave your job; told by the boss to leave
4. quit: decide to leave your job
5. intense: very great; extreme; too strong
6. praise: good things said about someone or something; compliments

Exercise 2 (page 33)

1. counter: the long table where you place your order at McDonald's
2. hire: give a job to someone
3. critics: people who have negative opinions about something or someone

Reading Selection 2: Technical Prose
"Language Mirrors Immigration, Provides Key to Nation's Past, Present"

Comprehension (pages 36–37)

1. F
2. T
3. F
4. F
5. T
6. F
7. Mon-Khmer
8. French Creole
9. F
10. F
11. T
12. European immigrants who came to the U.S. in the early 1900s are dying, and fewer European immigrants are entering the United States now.

13. California, New York, Florida
14. F
15. F
16. T
17. T
18. T
19. Indonesian is not one of the 25 languages (other than English) most commonly spoken in the United States.
20. Answers will vary.

Selection 3A: Trade Book
"Introduction"

Vocabulary from Context (pages 39–41)
1. spouses: marriage partners; husbands or wives
2. mother-in-law: the mother of one's spouse; colloquially, this term is sometimes used to describe the mother of one's partner whether or not one is married
3. stepchildren: spouse's children from a previous marriage
4. impression: feeling; sense; uncertain belief
5. adopt: to take someone into a family, especially used when children become legal members of a family that is not their biological family
6. guardian: a person who has legal responsibility for someone who cannot take care of him/herself, for example, an adult for a child
7. gay: homosexual; referring to people whose love/sexual relationships are with members of the same sex (Note, people often use the term *lesbians* to refer to homosexual women.)
8. commitment: promise
9. diversity: variety
10. acknowledgment: section of a book in which the author thanks those who have been of help; recognition or showing of a fact

Reading Selection 4: Technical Prose
"Marriage Taking a Back Seat"

Overview (page 52)
1. T
2. T
3. F
4. F

Comprehension (page 53)
1. F
2. F
3. F
4. T
5. F
6. F
7. F
8. T

Critical Reading (page 53)
Because most of the unmarried couples were younger, the assumption is that older people do marry. However, by referring to single people as people who have "not yet married," the article also might be seen as assuming that everyone will/should marry. People who are single by choice or who never marry might feel that this is an unfortunate choice of words because it can assume that being single is only a step on the way to marriage, not an adult way of life on its own. On the other hand, one might feel this is a statistically accurate description of the situation.

Discussion/Composition (pages 53–54)
1. For reasons why people choose not to marry, you might have thought of such things as wanting more time to oneself, wanting to pursue a career, being homosexual, not wanting children. The rest of this question calls for personal opinion.
2. This question calls for personal opinion.
3. As reasons for the decline in marriage age, you might have thought about the effects of industrialization—the fact that people were moving from farms into cities where they had more money and greater opportunity to meet partners. The marriage age probably rose in part because of the availability of higher education, especially to women. As advanced education has become more available, the average marriage age has increased.

Vocabulary from Context (page 54)
1. separation: when a married couple lives apart without legally ending the marriage
2. divorce: legal ending of a marriage
3. nuclear family: two biological parents and their children
4. arrangements: structure; organization; the way things are arranged
5. out of wedlock: her biological parents were not married to each other
6. widowed: to have had one's spouse die
7. delay: put off until later; postpone
8. decline: decrease; go down; lower
9. status: legal position
10. proportion: fraction

Reading Selection 5: Literature
Silas Marner

Comprehension (pages 56–57)
1. F
2. It was his only source of money; also, it filled up his days.
3. Silas was in his late thirties, but he looked like an old man.
4. 15 years
5. a, b, d (You might also have checked *f* because "love was not quite dead in his heart.")
6. F
7. a, b (This item is open to discussion. If you did not choose *a*, you might believe that Marner did not miss people.)
8. He moved his hands through the coins as if they were water.
9.    b.

Discussion (page 57)
2. Marner becomes part of the community because he adopts a child.

Vocabulary from Context (pages 57–59)
1. pounds and shillings: amounts of money
2. loom: a machine used to make cloth from thread or yarn
3. weaving: the act of making cloth on the loom
4. possession: something that belongs to someone
5. pleasures: things or events that please you, make you happy
6. satisfaction: a feeling of happiness or pleasure
7. memorial: an object that is intended to remind us of something or someone

8. boring: without interest, always the same

9. click: a sharp snapping sound, such as made when two hard objects are struck together

10. threads: thin strings made from wool or cotton, used to make cloth

11. celebration: a time of happiness and joy, usually in honor of someone or something

12. shutter: to pull closed wood that fits over windows, blocking out light and making the house safe

13. columns: vertical, round objects; cylinders

14. fond of: happy with, pleased with

Unit 3

Nonprose Reading: Campus Map

Part 1 (page 60)

1. 12
2. More Literate
3. More Sociable
4. This item is intended for discussion; the section you choose depends on your opinion.

Part 2 (pages 60–61)

5. The library is located in D3, on the East Mall. The bookstore is located in E3, on the East Mall.
6. The tennis courts are located in H2.
7. a. The East Mall leads directly from the library to the tennis courts.
   b. Probably not. There are no bus stops directly in front of the library or the tennis courts; however, you might use the bus stops at the Bus Loop (near the library) and the bus stops in front of either the University Hospital or Chris Spencer Pitch. However, this would not save you much walking.
   c. If you get hurt at the Tennis Bubble, you could go to the University Hospital, located in F2.
8. It appears that the restaurant closest to the hospital is the Old Barn Coffee Shop, just south of the hospital in F3. You might call Directory Assistance at 822-2211 or the Community Relations Office at 822-3131.
9. Yes.
10. F3. No. It appears that the road connecting the Main Library and the Old Barn Coffee shop is for pedestrians only.
11. Directory Assistance at 822-2211 or the Community Relations Office at 822-3131
12. a. 822-2211.
    b. On Saturday, directory assistance at UBC is not answered; you might try using a phone book or calling directory assistance for the city of Vancouver.

Word Study: Stems and Affixes

Exercise 1 (page 66)

1. a
2. television: an instrument that produces a picture of something that is far away (*tele:* far; *vis:* see) telegram: a written message sent far away (*tele:* far; *gram:* writing) transportation: the act of moving or carrying something from one place to another (*trans:* across; *port:* carry; *tion:* the act of)
3. For example, prepay, preread, preheat
4. presage: something that gives one knowledge of something before it happens; a warning

5. Immigration is the movement of people into a country; Emigration is the movement of people out of a country.
6. repaint, reuse, remake, reform, reborn, reread

Exercise 2 (pages 67–68)

1. vocal: singing; of or pertaining to the voice
2. portable: capable of being carried; easily carried or moved
3. transmit: to send from one place to another
4. videotape: to use a camera to make a tape of moving pictures that can be shown on television
5. porters: people whose job it is to carry suitcases for travelers
6. dictated: said or read material aloud for the purpose of having it recorded by a machine or written by a person
7. telephoto: of or related to a lens used to produce a large picture of something that is far away
8. imports: brings into the country
9. audiovisual: of or related to materials or equipment that present information so that it can be heard and seen
10. imposed: forced upon
11. inscribing: writing in the surface of something
12. manufactured: made; built
13. visualizing: seeing in his mind; imagining
14. autograph: a person's name written by that person; a signature
15. predictions: guesses about what will happen
16. prepay: pay ahead of time; pay before
17. remit: send back
18. emissions: what comes (is sent) out
19. spectators: people who were looking
20. edict: an official law or command of a ruler, often read out loud
21. dictator: a ruler who has total control of a country; people must do whatever the dictator says to do
22. deposed: removed from power; taken out of a position of power
23. evokes: calls forth; calls up; awakens
24. deforestation: the act of cutting down trees or forests
25. factory: a building in which products are made
26. inspectors: people who look at or examine something carefully, often looking for problems
27. televized: shown on television; made into a television program
28. remarried: married again
29. reapply: apply again; ask for admission again
30. de-ice: take the ice off of; remove the ice from
31. vista: view; scene

Word Study: Dictionary Use

Exercise 1 (pages 70–72)

1. It's always safe to use the first entry. However, in many dictionaries, unless indicated, all entries are acceptable.
2. two: dis-count; this dictionary uses a dot (·). When you reach the end of a line, you will want to hyphenate long words at the syllable divisions.
3. a. The first pronunciation has the stress on the first syllable.
4. Verb: 9; noun: 7
5. F (*discount* comes from French via Old French and Middle Latin.)
6. Derived words: words with related meaning that have been produced from the key word, as "discountable."
7. At the bottom of the page
   a. out
   b. at the beginning or the end of the dictionary

8. Answers will vary.
9. Usage labels help us know how, where, or if a word is used.
10. a. 16
    b. 2
    c. 5

Exercise 2 (pages 72–73)

1. a. T
   b. F
   c. F
2. four: cro/cid/o/lite
3. the first: *cron*yism
4. a. F (A crocus is a flower.)
   b. over
   c. the *a,* as in *a*lone
5. kro' sha
6. a. cropped
   b. crookedly
   c. cronies
7. F (He was English; he died in 1827.)
8. a. croissant: French
   b. cronk: Yiddish
   c. crochet: French
   d. crony: Greek
9. crop
10. a. 12 synonyms
    b. 0 antonyms

Sentence Study: Comprehension (pages 74–76)

1. a	4. d	7. c	10. b
2. d	5. a	8. c	11. a
3. b	6. b	9. a	12. a

Paragraph Reading: Restatement and Inference (pages 78–81)

1. b, c
2. a, d
3. c, d (Note: you may have checked *a.* This is reasonable if you believe that anyone who worries about how a napkin is folded is always neat and clean.)
4. b
5. b, d
6. b, c
7. a
8. b, c
9. d
10. c (Note, you may have also checked *a.* This is a reasonable guess. In fact, Helen Keller was a pacifist who did not believe in war; but one doesn't necessarily know this from the sentence.)

Discourse Focus: Careful Reading / Drawing Inferences (Mysteries) (pages 82–85)

1. "The Case of the Big Deal": Vance claimed he had a barber shave off "seven months of beard" the day before he met Haledjian. Yet his cheeks and chin were "tanned." If he had really been in the sun seven months without shaving, his chin would not have been suntanned.
2. "The Case of the Lying Gardener": A legal will could not be dated November 31. There are only 30 days in November.
3. "The Case of the Fake Robbery": The candles "dripped down the side facing the windows." If the window really had been left open as long as Mrs. Sidney said, some wax would have dripped on the other side, away from the direction of the wind.
4. "The Case of the Buried Treasure": If the pure silver candlestick had been lying in a bag from 1956 until "immediately" before Bertie took it to Haledjian, it would not have been "shining."
5. "The Case of the Dentist's Patient": Burton said he had never heard of Dr. Williams. If this were true, he would not have known the doctor was a dentist and a woman.

Unit 4

Reading Selection 1: Newspaper Article *"Farmer Calls Hole His Home"*

Comprehension (page 88)

1. F
2. F
3. F
4. F
5. T
6. F
7. F
8. F

Critical Reading (pages 88–89)

These questions call for your opinions.

Vocabulary from Context (pages 89–90)

1. bachelor: an unmarried man
2. trailer: mobile home; a vehicle used as a home; a home on wheels
3. shovels: tools used to dig earth or snow
4. ceiling: top of a room
5. skylight: a window in a roof that lets in light
6. concrete: a hard material used to build roads and buildings; it's made by mixing water, sand, and small rocks with a powder called cement. When these harden, the concrete becomes like stone.
7. storage: a place to keep things not currently being used
8. unconcerned: not concerned; free from worry; not caring about
9. affectionately: warmly; lovingly; showing that she likes them
10. favor: kind or helpful act
11. hermit: person who lives away from other people
12. mean: hateful; unkind

Reading Selection 2: Popular Social Science *"Lies Are So Commonplace, They Almost Seem Like the Truth"*

Comprehension

Exercise 1 (pages 92–93)
2, 3, 4, 5, 7, 8, 9

Exercise 2 (pages 93–94)
1. c (perhaps a)
2. d (perhaps c)
3. d, h
4. a, b
5. h
6. g (perhaps b)

Exercise 3 (page 94)
1. a. A
   b. A
   c. A

d. A
e. E
f. E
g. E
h. A
2. Probably not. This is not a scholarly or academic discussion of the subject.

Vocabulary from Context

Exercise 1 (page 95)
1. lies: untruths
2. fudge: tell small lies
3. claim: say; state
4. newborn: infant; baby who has just been born
5. do (lunch): have a meal together
6. leap: jump

Exercise 2 (page 96)
1. behaviors: actions
2. purposes: functions; ends; goals
3. avoid: keep from doing; keep away from
4. memory: what we remember; a remembrance
5. destroy: get rid of; kill; ruin
6. trust: belief in truthfulness; confidence

Selection 3A: Popular Social Science
"Who's Doing the Work around the House?"

Comprehension

Exercise 1 (pages 100–101)

TABLE 1. Sharing Tasks: Reports of Who Does Household Chores (%)

	Family Arrangement	
Who Does Chores	All Families (Women's reports)	Families in Which Both Spouses Work (Men's reports)
Women do nearly all	41	24
Women do most; husbands help	41	42
Task evenly divided	15	28
Husbands do more	2	5

TABLE 2. Sharing Money: Men's and Women's Reports When Both Work (%)

Salaries combined for all things	79
Some money kept separately	15

TABLE 3. Exchanging Roles: Respect for Stay-At-Home Husbands (%)

	Year		
Respect for the husband	1970	1980	Now
Would respect him less	63	41	25
Would respect him more	8	6	12
Would respect him the same	15	42	50

TABLE 4. Teenagers Sharing Chores (%)

	Chore					
Who Does Chore	Vacuum	Mop	Cook	Wash Dishes	Wash Car	Mow Lawn
Women's work	40	50	39	54	2	
Shared work	38		46		39	
Men's work		50	2	46	40	64
Doesn't matter who does it	20		13		19	

Exercise 2 (page 101)
1. T
2. T
3. F
4. F
5. T

Vocabulary from Context

Exercise 1 (pages 102–3)
1. chores: tasks; regular household jobs
2. gap: difference; separation
3. salaries: money paid for working; earnings
4. expenses: costs; bills; money owed
5. roles: jobs; functions; responsibilities
6. attitudes: feelings; point of view
7. generation: period of time between the birth of parents and the birth of their children; people born at the same time
8. have less respect for: think less of; have a lower opinion of; have less regard for; have less esteem for
9. child-rearing: taking care of children; raising children; bringing up children; child care
10. responsibility: duty; job
11. disciplining: correcting; training; punishing

Exercise 2 (page 103)
1. savings
2. the norm
3. breadwinners
4. likely

5. duty
6. primarily
7. are determined
8. significance
9. newfound

Selection 3B: Cartoons
"Sally Forth" (pages 104–6)

Monday
1. Sally wants them both to know how much work the other does ("how big a load the other is carrying") so they will recognize the importance of what one another does ("won't take each other for granted").
2. Ted will wash the dishes; Sally will read about sports in the newspaper.

Tuesday
1. Ted is doing the laundry.
2. He doesn't want to have to clean it up (which Sally usually does).

Wednesday
1. Ted is cleaning the house.
2. Ted is complaining ("nagging") about Sally's not cleaning up after herself; Sally seems to be giving a speech she has heard from Ted about not being able to change.

Thursday
1. Ted is loading the dishwasher.
2. Ted is starting to become angry because others are doing the things that he usually does (like not putting his dirty dishes in the dishwasher). His annoyance (or the fact that he sounds just like Sally usually does in the same situation) tells their daughter that Sally and Ted really have changed roles and, perhaps, he has learned something.

Friday
1. Yes and no. Ted says that switching roles has "opened [his] eyes." At the same time, he still expects Sally to make him breakfast while he reads the newspaper.
2. Ted still expects to be able to read the newspaper while Sally makes breakfast.

Selection 3C: Magazine Article
"The 'New Father': No Real Role Reversal"

Comprehension (page 108)
1. F
2. T
3. F
4. F
5. The author seems to feel that parents need to find an arrangement that meets both of their individual needs.

Vocabulary from Context

Exercise 1 (page 110)
1. involvement: participation; taking part in
2. child-rearing: taking care of children; raising children; bringing up children; child care
3. responsibility: duties; involvement
4. roles: jobs; functions; responsibilities
5. status: position; rank; place in society; standing
6. privilege: special right or power

7. penalty: punishment; disadvantage; loss; hardship
8. arrangements: structures; organizations; the way things are arranged

Exercise 2 (page 111)
1. satisfied
2. participation
3. overlooked
4. child-caring
5. suits

Reading Selection 4: Magazine Graphic
"Summit to Save the Earth: The World's Next Trouble Spots"

Getting Oriented (page 113)
1. Air Pollution; Population Growth; Safe Drinking Water; Protected Lands
2. By location: North America; Latin America; Europe; Africa; Asia and Oceania

Grading the World (pages 114–16)
1. a. This calls for your opinion.
   b. F (number of births compared with size of population = % increase in population)
   c. In general, the earth must be protected from humans.
   d. This calls for your opinion.
2. F
3. This calls for your opinion.
4. F
5. T
6. F
7. Ecuador and Argentina
8. This calls for your opinion.
9. This calls for your opinion.
10. Protected Lands received 7 F's, followed by Safe Drinking Water, with 5.
11. U.S., Canada, Australia
12. F
13. This calls for your opinion.

Reporting on the World (page 116)
1. T
2. T
3. a. This calls for your opinion. The government is cleaning 23 miles of river, but critics say this is for the diamond industry, not for drinking water.
   b. T (Clearing the forests creates farmland today, but the land may not be usable in the future.)
   c. We do not know what will happen. If cutting down of the forests continues, this will be true.
4. Mining, logging, tourism, and overgrazing of cattle and sheep.
5. F, but they are working on it.
6. This calls for your opinion.

Vocabulary from Context

Exercise 1 (pages 120–21)
1. population: number of people
2. environmental: having to do with the environment; concerning the land, water, and air surrounding the earth.
3. summits: high-level meetings
4. industrialization: the growth of industry, of factories and machinery

5. economies: the system of business, farm, and labor that produces money for a country
6. polluted: filled with dangerous chemicals or gases
7. toxic: dangerous; poisonous
8. chemical waste: unused or unusable liquids from factories
9. dammed: stopped rivers or streams for human use
10. lumber: wood taken from trees and used in building houses
11. timber: wood; lumber
12. clear-cut: to cut all of the trees down
13. erosion: the washing or wearing away of soil by water
14. rate: speed
15. threatened: in danger (of being hurt or damaged)
16. displaced: forced to move
17. damage: hurt; injury
18. trash: garbage; paper, metal, plastic, etc., that people do not use up.

19. disposing: putting away; putting in a safe place
20. balance: equal weight on two sides
21. hunters: people who kill animals
22. wild: living in forests or deserts, away from people
23. tropical: warm, wet parts of the world
24. rare: uncommon; not easily found
25. extinct: no longer on earth; killed out completely
26. protect: to save from harm
27. preserves: safe places for animals
28. quality of life: amount of comfort and health in living

Exercise 2 (page 122)
1. marine sanctuary
2. fragile
3. scarred
4. overgrazing